W9-CPN-439

WHITE WATER

ALSO BY JOYCE REISER KORNBLATT

Nothing to Do with Love,
STORIES 1981

WHITE WATER

Joyce Reiser Kornblatt

E. P. DUTTON, INC. ▪ NEW YORK

*A portion of this novel appeared, in slightly different form,
in* The Atlantic Monthly *(August 1984).*

Published in the United States by
E. P. Dutton, Inc.,
2 Park Avenue, New York, N.Y. 10016

Library of Congress Cataloging in Publication Data
Kornblatt, Joyce Reiser.
White water.
I. Title.
PS3561.0662W5   1985   813'.54
85-1606

ISBN: 0-525-24313-5

Published simultaneously in Canada
by Fitzhenry & Whiteside Limited, Toronto

Designed by Nancy Etheredge

10 9 8 7 6 5 4 3 2 1

First Edition

For my family

ROSE

DID HE THINK I wouldn't come?

Sending me the money like that. I called him right up long distance and not even past eleven when the rates are low. "Now Karl," I said, "did you think I wouldn't come to my own granddaughter's wedding? And what do you mean, putting one-hundred-dollar bills in the mail like that? Don't you know the risk on that, don't you watch the news anymore in Florida?"

He said, "You can't live in fear, Mother."

He sounded just like his father did. Certain as a preacher. As if he knew better than anyone exactly how the world worked, but he would be patient with the rest of us who weren't so blessed in the intelligence department.

"I'm still living in Washington, D.C., remember? We have plenty to be afraid of here. Mail robberies, for one."

"You received the money, Mother."

"This time I did. And that is not even my point. My point is, did you think I wouldn't come? Else why would you send me plane fare, Karl, which you know I can afford better than you?"

"Mother," he said, "a person on a fixed income is never better off than a person with earning power. We're having a good season here, which is the same for me as getting a raise if I still worked in government. You don't get raises from pension funds."

"Please remember my stock dividends."

I don't like it when he makes out that his father didn't leave me well-provided for. Karl will never directly attack Wendell—not like Justin will, I mean—but sometimes Karl comes in the side door, quiet, his words skulking around you while you're not paying attention and next time you look up, *bam!*—something's been stolen from you. I feel it the same as if it were my Zenith portable color TV or the sterling silver candlesticks I keep in the corner cupboard with the Noritake china— not that it's the finest line, it isn't, but it's my treasure all the same.

"All the same," Karl was saying, "I want you to have the money, Mother. I'll meet you at the airport. You just let me know when you'll be arriving."

[4]

"I can tell you that right now," I said. "Tomorrow at one in the afternoon. I bought my ticket yesterday at the Riviera Travel Agency, right next to my eye doctor's, where I was for my glaucoma test. I guess you can see I'm on my toes all right."

"Bring enough clothes to stay for a week," he instructed. "I want you to stay for a good week. I want you to spend some time with Charlotte and me. And Mary, of course."

Charlotte is Karl's second wife and Mary is her retarded daughter, twenty or so, but babbles like a child and I think she might wear diapers, too. Think of it. I told Charlotte once, "I imagine your heart breaks every day of your life," but she said, "No, Rose, Mary is my blessing, my sweet gift from heaven." This is what Karl's loaded onto himself now, after all his trouble with Florence. I would have thought he'd want some peace, but he never is attracted to the normal things; he's always coming at life sideways, where an ordinary person would look at a situation straight on and say, "Thank you, but no thank you." Not that he isn't a practical man, he is. Up here he made it to G.S. 12, and he does run the motel now in Florida, which takes a good head for detail work. But on personal matters he's just not very sharp. At least that has been my opinion.

After Karl, I called up Justin. He only lives twenty minutes away by car, or half an hour on the T-4 bus, but I could have been calling Miami again, for all the time I see him.

"What a shock," I said when he answered. "You're home."

"No," he said. "Actually, this is a recording of my voice. Would you care to leave a message for me when I return?"

"Justin, do your jokes in a night club where they'll pay you for rudeness. What I'm calling to ask you is, Are you going this weekend to Diana's wedding?"

I heard a sharp hissing sound on the receiver, which was Justin letting out a breath like he does when he's upset. You'd think he was one of those life-size blow-up toys sometimes, all the hissing he does—or maybe he was striking a match. Which wouldn't have been any better, worse even, because it wouldn't have been any regular cigarette he'd be lighting. It would be that dope.

"Didn't know she was getting married," he said, and I could tell from his voice he was either hurt or lying—it had a hollowed-out sound, which comes from squeezing the real feeling out of your words before you say them, so as they come out empty and false.

"It's hard for me to believe your own brother wouldn't invite you to—"

"It's hard for you to believe most things about your family," he answered. "You are still working so hard at 'Father Knows Best,' when actually—"

I didn't want to hear about Justin's notion of actual. He picks out the worst examples and passes them off as the whole picture, and he is so good with words—I don't mean just what he says, I mean the way he puts a thing across, which of course he was trained to do in law school. Well, you start to wonder if life isn't as ugly as he makes it out to be. He can be a mean-spirited boy. Neither his father nor me was bad-tempered, at least I wouldn't paint us that way. And Karl, of course, is generous to a fault, except when he's overtired and then he gets a little snappish is all. But Justin. The way he carried on at Wendell's funeral. Oh. That scene stayed with me for months: Wendell's body laying so peaceful in Toomer Brothers' Funeral Parlor, they had him fixed up so nice, and Justin coming over to the casket and— I don't let myself remember it anymore. No. Right now a curtain's come down in my mind, like when Mr. Fred Toomer brought down the coffin lid on Wendell.

"Don't insult me, Justin," I said on the phone. "I am still your mother."

"You haven't always behaved like one," my youngest child said to me.

Imagine. But it doesn't affect me like it used to. It used to give me dizzy spells. I would have to go and lie down for an hour after one of Justin's outbursts. Then Grace explained it to me one day: "He has tantrums, Rose. It's like part of him never grew up. In that place he's still two years old." Grace is Justin's former wife, but she never has remarried. I don't think she even sees other men, though she's pretty as Doris Day, and I think sometimes they even spend the night together. And two beautiful children.

Maybe it's my heart that breaks every day of my life.

"I'll give everyone your best, Justin," I said.

He gave a little hoot and hung up.

The closest I ever got to getting on an airplane while Wendell was alive was when we started going Sunday afternoons to the travelogues at the Smithsonian Institution. (Some of my West Virginia relations came to visit once and I said, "We are going to take you to the Smithsonian Institution," and Cousin Albert said he'd always thought that was a nuthouse for politicians. They are backward in West Virginia.) In the travelogues, each one began with pictures of the clouds above whichever country we were visiting that day. We flew into Greece, Italy, England, Sweden, France, Hong Kong, Hawaii and Madagascar like that, which was good enough for Wendell, seeing how he lived in his head entirely, but I have got to touch and smell and brush up against a place before I'm satisfied I've been there. Which is what I guess is meant by "down to earth." You want to feel the grit between your toes is all.

In planes, you can cover more ground. I always hankered to travel by plane. Not Wendell. "If God had wanted us to fly . . ." he'd say. You know the rest. "Wendell," I'd answer, "you can say that about anything. Clothing, for example." He wouldn't budge. Every summer we went by train or bus on a one-week excursion to some educational place. Hershey, Pa., or Williamsburg, or Princeton, New Jersey. Wendell wanted the boys to go to Princeton. He reasoned that if he exposed them in their youth to the feel of the place, they'd have it in their systems when the time came for them to go off to college. Of course, they didn't. Karl went to the University of Maryland, rode the bus every day from home, took his lunch in a paper bag and worked weekends in a 7-11 store. And Justin went to six colleges before he graduated. His academic career was like one of those progressive dinners they used to have when I was growing up in Berkeley Springs, each course at a different house. You'd travel as much as you'd eat. Law school he did in one place, Howard University, right in Washington, but of course he didn't live at home. "Howard's for Negroes," Wendell complained. "Why would he choose a Negro school?"

"Because," I said, "he's Justin Fry."

Which was answer enough for me, but for Wendell that suggested a bigger question than the one he'd asked. Wendell was never much good at taking a person for how he was. "The object of life," Wendell would say, "is the struggle toward perfection." I think he got that from Bishop Fulton J. Sheen, who he watched on television all the time. Wendell meant *his* struggle toward everybody *else's* perfection, which I don't think is what Bishop Sheen had in mind.

Four years ago, after Wendell was already gone, I rode the plane for the first time, going down to Florida for Karl's hernia operation. Not exactly what I'd longed for all those years. But life has a way of delivering the goods too late, damaged, the wrong size or color, or after you remember why you ordered the thing in the first place. Doesn't it? I'd have just as soon been on a Greyhound, for all the pleasure I got from that flying trip. Worrying all the way down about Karl's condition. He was already divorced from Florence and not yet married to Charlotte, so who did he have to fall back on but me, his mother? All the way down I chewed Chiclets and held on to the paper bag they give you for vomiting. Four times I read that card about oxygen and life jackets, but I know I would have passed out before I'd had a chance to save myself. All I could think was: *Wendell, you were right; this is not what God intended after all.*

"You must be mistaken," I told the taxi driver. "This couldn't be my son's address."

"I took you where you tol' me, leddy."

In the rearview mirror, I could see his face. "Are you related to Desi Arnaz?" I said, thinking if I complimented him he'd be more likely to help me track down Karl.

But he tapped his finger against the meter. "Three dollahs and twenny-fi' cens." He looked just like Desi does getting stern with Lucy. I had to laugh. He whipped around and glared at me through the glass partition.

"Don't mek jokes," he said. "Don't mek jokes on me, leddy."

I gave him the money plus tip, and carried my Samsonite Tourister by myself up to the front porch of the Beach Haven Inn. It was no haven that I could see. Three rows of old people on folding chairs and everybody looking at the ocean as if it were the grave itself. One man without teeth, a portable radio in his lap and he was listening to horse races, but I don't think he could have cheered if he'd had a million dollars riding on the winner. He was all worn out. They all were. Even the Inn sagged and groaned like it wanted to fall down in a heap on the sand.

"No rooms," the lady on the chair right by the front door said to me. Her face was closing up on itself like one of those Japanese parchment fans, her white hair had thinned so I could see her baby-pink scalp, and her voice was so faint, I thought: *This woman is disappearing right before my eyes.* It's how Wendell went, an inch at a time, everything shrinking except his ears. How he suffered.

"I'm not looking for a room," I said. "I'm looking for my son, Karl Fry, but I don't think—"

"Second floor," she said. She pointed upwards with her whole hand like she was taking an oath. "He's next to me. Nice boy, Karl Fry."

Imagine. My firstborn actually resided in this halfway house—halfway between living and not—and it smelled more like Toomer Brothers' than any inn any day. I smelled it soon as I walked through the door. Something like rotten flowers, carnations left over from some long-past celebration, all the petals shriveled up, the stems gone slimy and brown. It near to knocked me out. I had to set myself on the turquoise vinyl love seat in the lobby, and the plastic whooshed under my weight; you could have mistaken the sound for you-know-what-which-ladies-do-not-do. The desk clerk peered at me over his glasses, one side of his mouth hitched up into a grin. I thought I'd expire.

"May I help you?" he said. The grin was gone from his face, which was moon round and just as pale. A pale person stands out more in Florida, what with all those suntans and Cubans. His hair was slicked back with that pomade like they used in the forties. Wendell used it, parted his jet black hair and oiled it shiny as a helmet. I used to say, "Wendell, you look like Clark Gable when you fix your hair like that," which of course he didn't, but it would soften him some.

Carefully I rose up from the love seat, and luckily for me it did not make a noise this time. I said, "Can you tell me where I can find Karl Fry? I don't suppose he's in his room at present."

"No, m'am," he said. He was Pledging the counter while he talked. You had the feeling this lobby was as far as he ever went and he kept everything in it clean as a mausoleum. "Karl works down the beach aways," he went on. "At the Eden Roc Hotel. You can't miss it. Looks like the Taj Mahal. You be a relation of his?"

"I'm his mother," I said. "I guess you can't be more related than that."

At the Eden Roc, Karl was learning hotel management "on the job," he said. They had him being everything from bell hop to desk clerk to dishwasher in the restaurant. I wouldn't be surprised to know he did a turn with the chambermaids, scrubbing out toilet bowls and picking up dirty tissues from underneath the beds.

"Karl," I said, "I don't see why they don't give you a management position. In D.C. you made it to G.S. 12."

"Now, Mother," Karl was saying, "I'm having to learn the business firsthand this way. This is better than a college degree."

A forty-year-old man carrying rich people's suitcases. Smiling, smiling, smiling. Chintzy tips. And him with government service under his belt, and four years at the state university; all those A's in political science and accounting and Principles of Management I and II. And living in a rooming house to boot.

Well, that was four years ago. Things have improved some. He's married to Charlotte now and they have their own place near the ocean, twenty minutes from Miami Beach. Fry's Lodge, they call it. Along the road, there's signs what say FRY'S LODGE, so-many MILES, and a finger pointing south.

After the third finger, a sign says, FRY'S LODGE: YOU'RE HERE AT LAST! I must admit it's good psychology. Makes you feel you've been looking for the place most of your life.

Karl eases the jeep along the gravel drive into the parking space between the main house and the redwood fence that divides his property from the highway.

"You drive this vehicle like a real outdoorsman," I say. "You drive it like a pro."

Actually, Karl drives the jeep like Wendell drove our '49 DeSoto, which he kept running for eighteen years. I'd say, "Wendell, we look like some exhibit let loose from the Museum of Science and Technology; we look like antiques instead of modern people," but he would not part with that DeSoto. I can see him now, hunched over the wheel like an old man with bad vision, or someone caught in a downpour and not hardly able to see the next bend in the road, or the signs that say DANGER. SLOW DOWN. SHARP TURN AHEAD.

"Nice of you to say that, Mother," Karl says. (I'm glad to see I've bolstered him some.) "I do feel at home down here."

He passes his eyes over the main house, which is a two-story stucco in dire need of painting, and the six scruffy cabins, plopped down on the sandy soil like they fell out of a plane and were lucky enough to land right-side up, but not much more than that. In terms of a plan, I mean. In terms of landscaping and such. In front of the main house, I see a camellia bush or two, and this cheers me some. Maybe they have a garden in back, at least. I am a lover of gardens, even if I have spent all the years since I married living in an apartment building on Connecticut Avenue, one of the busiest streets in Washington, D.C. Still, I would like to give Karl some gardening advice—I learned it all as a girl, from my Daddy—but I know how Karl would respond. Oh, he wouldn't be belligerent. No. That's Justin's talent. As a boy, Karl would sit quiet and polite, nodding his head while I talked, blinking his eyes fast like he does when he's concentrating, like they were machines taking dictation, recording in code every word I said. But when I'd finish with my advice, he'd lean back, give his lids a rest, then say, "Well, Mother, I will surely give that some thought," and go on doing whatever he intended to do in the first place. Finally I stopped being helpful.

"Look," he says now. "There's Mary."

She's in a hammock hooked to poles in front of the house. She is so excited to see us, she starts thrashing like a beached fish and before we have gotten out of

[14]

the jeep, she's all tangled up in the mesh. She can't figure out the simplest tasks. Charlotte tried to teach her how to knit, for example, but it was too much for poor Mary. She broke the needles in half, threw the yarn in the garbage, then cut up the afghan I made them for their sofa because it reminded her of her defeat. "I hope it doesn't hurt your feelings, Rose," Charlotte had written me. "She didn't mean anything against you. She lost her temper at herself." People think the feebleminded don't realize their situation, but they do. Of course they do. I think all of us are born with a picture in our heads of our ideal selves, and everything we do or fail to do is measured against that possibility. Take me, for instance. Haven't I always known I should be Rose Fry, book writer? Don't I tell a story good enough to hold still a roomful of ladies all wound up like they get before Thursday night Bingo at St. Bartholomew's Church? Don't they always say, "Rose, you should send that into *Reader's Digest*. They pay big money for material like that."

"Mary," Karl says, helping her right herself, holding the hammock still while she gets down, "here is your grandmother Rose. Can you give a hello to your grandmother Rose?"

"Ha-low," she says in that stretched-out way she has of talking, like every syllable is an effort for her, or a sound she savors—I'm not able to figure out which.

"Hello, Mary," I say and give her a peck on the cheek. Look what she does: claps her hands like I just did a magic trick, like I just turned a cartwheel. It strikes me suddenly that in this way she resembles Karl—get-

[15]

ting delight from the smallest things, pumping them up, failing to aspire to the bigger opportunities in life.

"Well, Mother," Karl says as we walk toward the house, "what do you think of our place?"

"Beautiful," I tell him. "Surely impressive." When actually I'm thinking: *Karl Fry, why do you always set your sights so low?*

"Thank you, Charlotte," I say.

She's brought me a glass of lemonade while Karl goes upstairs with my bags. I had forgotten what a nice-looking woman she is. Puts me in mind of Katharine Hepburn in *The African Queen*. Something composed in her even in the middle of the jungle, and I don't mean make-up that doesn't streak. Florence always looked neat as a pin and, feature by feature, she's prettier than Charlotte. But Florence always struck me as right on the verge of spoiling, or drying out, like bread exposed too long to the air.

I'm sitting at the kitchen table in the fan's hot breeze. "Air-conditioning's down again," Charlotte says, unfazed. She's making the salad we'll have with our supper. Mary is sitting tailor-seat on the floor, like a child, looking at pictures of jungle animals in *National Geographic*. I sip my drink and try to think of something else to say.

What I'm thinking is: *Karl Fry, married twice, who'd have believed it?* I used to fear he'd never have a date, let alone two wives and alimony and what they call these days "blended families," which means nobody is sure how they're related or for how long.

"Oh, Charlotte, before I forget, I want to give you these baby pictures I found of Karl."

She puts the salad in the fridge and sits down with me at the table. It's so warm my fingers stick to the photographs. I have to peel them, like a child's hands, from my skin. She lifts a picture up, gently, by the edges. Holds it like a treasure. Her eyes mist over. "What a gentle face," she says.

Even as a baby, he was timid. Some cry with gusto. Even before they have words, they're announcing: *I mean for you to pay attention to me.* Not Karl. From the start he seemed to apologize for his presence. People would tell me, "Rose, you're so lucky to have a good one instead of one that fusses all the time," but I was uneasy for him. Good ones lose their places in line. They never learn to push and shove like everybody else; they wait longer for less. At least this has been my experience.

"Gentle is one way to name it," I say. "His father never did adjust to that."

"Karl rarely mentions him," Charlotte says.

I recognize that appeal in her eyes. I sent the same message to my own mother-in-law: *What hides in his silence? What secrets does he have that he can't share?* Florence never wanted to know anything I might pass on to her. She was all closed doors and lights out early.

"Wendell did not take to having a shy boy," I tell Charlotte.

He wanted his son to play team sports, speak up in class, join Cub Scouts, church choir, get in trouble some, like other children do. He would sit Karl down for "pep talks," and Karl would pretend to listen like he does, but I knew it was a waste of time. "Listen, Wendell," I would tell him later. "Karl's not up to it—he doesn't have the wherewithal."

"A child needs to be shaped, Rose," he'd counter. "A boy takes to guidance and direction."

Wendell was a real believer in slow progress. At the F.B.I., he worked in Fingerprints and he could spend months combing through records, trying to match up prints on file with those on stolen cars or automatic pistols or phony fifty-dollar bills. "Persistence pays off nine times out of ten," he'd say, and Karl's shyness turned into one more case for Wendell to crack. "We'll get to the bottom of it yet," he was still announcing when Karl was in high school and keeping to himself as much as ever.

"There's no bottom to get to," I'd say. "Maybe he likes the way he is. Maybe he's content."

I am telling this all to Charlotte, as I remember it, dreaming aloud my family's past. "You were wise," Charlotte says. She looks at Mary. "To accept him for himself."

I had come to that hard, I have to admit. Even though I didn't believe that Karl could be shaped, directed and guided out of his own personality as if it were a bad habit or an allergy he'd outgrow, I kept checking him over for signs of loneliness the way other mothers look for head lice or athlete's foot. "Oh, Charlotte, I worried over him plenty. It wasn't just Wendell who wasn't easy about Karl's nature."

Once when he was thirteen or so, he said, "Mother, I am not a lame animal in your care."

That was the first time I had ever heard him speak up on his own behalf. Even though it was at my expense, I wondered: *Is this the breakthrough Wendell's worked for all these years?*

"I had no intention to insult you, Karl," I said, but already he was backsliding. There were real tears in his eyes. He said, "I'm sorry, Mother. I didn't mean to hurt your feelings."

"Karl," I said, and I sat down with him at the kitchen table where he was eating his Temple orange, section by section, neat as a girl; all the peel piled on a napkin, another one handy to wipe his fingers, dab at the juice on his chin. "Karl, lately I've noticed you haven't been coming straight home from school, and I am wondering what you do with yourself on those days. Seeing how you don't seem inclined to mix much. Seeing how you're not interested in friends."

I pictured him standing alone at the edge of the playground, watching the others cavort. Once, during recess, I'd walked to his school and hidden in the shrubs that bordered the blacktop lot where all the others joined in soccer games and Red Rover and the like. My son sat by himself in the shade, reading a book. Maybe after school he was hiding in a tree in Rock Creek Park while groups of children tore across the grass and shouted themselves hoarse from all the fun they were having.

"I do have friends," he said. "That's what I've been doing. Visiting my friends."

I clutched at my collar. "Well, who? Who?" Maybe Wendell's experiment had paid off after all! "I'm not acquainted with any of your—"

"Yes, you are." He offered me an orange section, but I declined. "Mr. Calabrese and Mr. Blum. And John Peabody at the zoo. He's a herpetolgist."

"Those are adults, Karl. I thought you said 'friends.' "

"Adult friends. I prefer them. I learn from them. I—"

"From Mr. Calabrese? From a shoemaker? What—"

Then he imitated Mr. Calabrese, and he had that Italian accent down to a tee. "I vill tell you about my con-tree. Not the Hollywood baloney, not the gangster lies. My con-tree is Si-ci-lee. Leesen. To leave your native con-tree, it is like cutting off one foot, all the rest of life you hobble."

Now I tell Charlotte, "It shut me up. His face was glowing like he'd just won a Little League pennant."

She smiles. She knows that look.

"Mr. Blum's interesting, too," he went on. You would have thought he was auditioning for the eighth grade play or going out for the debating team. "I asked him what he liked about being a baker and he said, 'Karl, what you learn from baking is patience. It's a great teacher of patience. So long to rise, so long to bake, so long to cool. It gives a good perspective.' "

"But—" That's all I said: But.

"But what, Mother?" he said.

I couldn't answer that one, no sir. "Who is this John Peabody?" I said. "What did you say he did?"

"Herpetologist," Karl said. "Snakes. Sometimes he lets me hold them. By the head. As if you were grasping a garden hose." He held up his index finger and grabbed it with his other hand to demonstrate.

"I'll remember that," I said, "if I'm ever stranded in the Everglades."

At that moment Justin knocked over a lamp in the parlor. We could hear the glass shatter on the hardwood floor. Justin was eight then, normal as any hurricane that might blow through your life, hundred-mile winds and damage no insurance covers. You know how they write it down in the policies: "We are not responsible for acts of God."

So I left my strange, tidy, quiet son and went to clean up Justin's latest wreckage.

After that, I began to see Karl in a new light. I felt less fearful that he'd make it through, is what I mean. But in my bones, I knew, like a mother does, that he would never be at home in the everyday world. He would always live in a place apart. He'd be different, not like average people, even if he stayed in their midst forever.

But Charlotte and I can't talk anymore. Karl's on the stairs, we hear the boards creaking under his adult weight. I realize she's taken hold of my hand. Maybe all the time I spoke to her of Karl, she held it like this.

Charlotte's saying, "Rose, I understand Florence has planned a lovely party for Saturday," meaning the wedding, and I'd like to bring up Justin to her, the fact of his absence, but Karl's in the kitchen now and I get shy again. All the way from the airport I tried out versions in my mind: *Isn't it a shame that Justin couldn't make it down with me?* or *Justin certainly will regret not seeing Diana get married, he always had a special fondness for her as a child,* or just straight out asking, *Did you or did you not invite your brother to this wedding?*

But I don't ask it straight or roundabout. I don't because I know the answer, knew it soon as I hung up with Justin on the phone: he had not been invited and if he had, he wouldn't have come. Between my boys lies the Gulf of Mexico and I am a poor swimmer in those waters. It's enough for me to put my toe in from time to time and remind myself how deep it goes, how strong the undercurrents and how they could pull you down in no time flat. Justin's wrong. It isn't "Father Knows Best" I'm after, I gave that script up long ago. I am not a sentimentalist. No. I just want my sons to love each other is all.

I told that to Karl years ago when Justin had his perjury trial and Karl said, "Mother, love appears between people, it can't be willed. It isn't like losing weight or taking up calisthenics. Love appears, and the only decision you make is whether to invite love in or turn it away."

That boy. He makes everything sound religious. Sometimes I wonder if those years we counted him withdrawn, he wasn't praying instead.

Even the way he touches Charlotte now, his hands weightless on her damp shoulders, the kind of touch a priest gives, or the nuns at Mercy Hospital where Wendell died, who wasn't even Catholic himself. But he would quiet down whenever Sister Clare or Sister Jean Marie would lay a palm across his forehead; their fingers took his pain away, like sponges soak up water, naturally, with no special effort, simply the work they were intended to do. Does Charlotte grow cooler when Karl touches her like this? The hem on her sundress billows in the fan's breeze and Karl's trouser cuffs stir. My son and his wife seem to be rising before me, levitating, leaving behind the hot linoleum on which Mary sits, lost in her pictures of antelopes and giraffes. Now my body's lifting, too, I—

"Mother!" Karl rushes to my side. "What's wrong?"

"Just a little lightheaded," I whisper. I've nearly fainted, it appears, toppled forward on my earthbound chair. "Just the shock of the climate here, the heat and all." Charlotte brings a cool cloth for my head—*Oh, Wendell, I'm sorry I couldn't do for you what the Sisters could!*—and helps me to my bed where I sleep until morning, knocked out by love. At my age. What an embarrassment.

Last night I dreamed about who I was before I was Wendell's wife.

I have never had any trouble understanding how a person could pick up in the middle of a life, disappear from his neighborhood, move across the country and never look back at the past again. Women do this all the time when they get married. Yes. They drop their girlhoods behind them like so much extra freight and call themselves Mrs. Whoever and bob their hair. The past wiggles away like half of a severed worm. Miracle or mutilation, which is it?

In the dream, I was back again in Berkeley Springs, West Virginia. My mother raised me in a farmhouse two miles down the road from the Lodge, where she worked. She gave massages to the people who came there—they still do—for the famous mineral baths. George Washington visited there. Mama talked as if it were she, Esther Scruggs Temple herself, who helped him down into the healing water.

"George Washington," she'd announce, "put us on the map." This from a woman who worked for an hourly wage, collected tips in her pocket like a waitress or worse, came home exhausted every day and soaked her own hands in a solution she made from Epsom salts; her joints hurt so from all those hours she kneaded backs and shoulders, soothing the aches and pains of well-off ladies from D.C. or Charleston. Mama crowed about George Washington as if she were the proprietress of the establishment. It gave her a sense of dignity that the work itself did not provide. It gave her a place in history by association. But then she'd go on about how he had had this lumbago and all, and how he'd come to Berkeley Springs with this assistant or that, but never with Martha—"It appears they didn't get on so well," she'd confide—and even what he'd eaten for breakfast, lunch and supper during his stay.

She made it all up. He did come, true, but I don't think the Lodge was even there at the time, only the baths. All the details Mama just plain invented. She did the same about my father's death at Harpers Ferry, where the three of us had gone for a Sunday excursion. I was five years old at the time. Afterwards, I would hear her describe the way he'd plunged into the water to save a drowning child and perished himself. Actually, my father dropped off a bridge in full view of my mother and me, and disappeared forever into the Shenandoah.

"Mama," I'd say, "why don't you tell the truth about my father?"

She would fix her glare on me. "What do you know about truth? You were only five years old. You were a baby. What could a baby remember anyhow?"

Everything, I'd think. More than I'd care to.

Finally, when she was old, she said, "He put up a good front. Window dressing."

Here I'd pressed her all these years for explanations, reasons, a truth in which my sorrow could retire. She gave me harsher news than I wanted.

"That's your opinion," I said. "I think it was the fire blight."

Daddy raised Rome Beauties, Winesaps and McIntosh. While he was alive, my mother sold the fruit from a roadside stand she operated in front of our house. She sold cider she pressed herself, filled gallon jugs with a siphon from the vat that rested on the newspaper-covered wooden floor in the kitchen. I remember the smell of that tart perfume like another person knows her mother's cologne. Off-season, Daddy drove a backhoe for a builder in town, did carpentry jobs for neighbors, but if you asked him what his work was, he would tell you, "I have the finest orchard in Morgan County."

"Think what you like," Mama said. "It's all water over the dam."

If so, I'm still swimming in those white-frothed currents.

Mama and I are on the front porch, shelling peas. It's mid-April. Dogwoods and azaleas and all the spring bulbs ablaze.

"Fire blight," Daddy says.

When she sees him standing there with that blackened branch, the pods in Mama's lap clatter across the weathered floor, she is on her feet that fast.

"All my McIntosh have it," he says. He sinks down on the bottom porch step, his forehead to his knees, his shoulders quaking like he's chilled, like he's the one who's sick instead of his trees. I've never seen him sad before.

"A farmer's life is always risky," Mama says. She is still on the porch, and if she had a pulpit in front of her, she could pass for a lady preacher. Her arms are stretched out wide, and one of them pushes me back toward the glider when I make a move for the steps. "Nature does not promise us—"

"Damn it, Esther!" He cracks the branch in two across his knee and heaves the pieces into the yard. Withered blossoms scatter like ash over the lawn. This action empowers him again. He's on his feet, full height. "If I wanted an agriculture lecture, I'd call up the extension service!" He stomps off for the road I'm not allowed to cross. The orchard's on the other side. At the front yard's edge, he turns around. "Don't you know how to give a little comfort to a man?"

Mama's arms collapse. Her mouth gapes, but no sound comes out, just air. She looks the way a fish does when it's caught. She forgets about me and charges into the house, pea pods squashed beneath her stride. Through the screen door, I hear her clomping up the stairs and then the door to their bedroom slams and who is left to comfort him but me?

It seems I fly the span from the porch to orchard, avoiding altogether that deliberate and forbidden trek I must have made through the grass and over that graveled road, where cars and trucks and tractors passed our property all day long. I am in that grove is all I know. Up and down the dappled paths that run the length of the orchard, I hunt for him. I'm halfway down a blighted row—those trees look like they've been in a fire, yet nothing burned away—when I see him, straddling a high limb, his arms hugging the ruined bark. "Daddy!" I call to him. Before he can right himself, I have started up the ladder. Each rung's a whole leg span for me, but I am climbing like my feet have springs in them, and fear is no greater than a tickle in my throat.

"Rosie, good Christ, how—? Now watch yourself, be careful—"

He does not order me down. He's glad I've come. He guides me up, up to where he is, hoists me himself from ladder to branch, and when I'm there beside him on that perch, his arm holding me secure, it isn't fire blight I see this close to sky, but dazzle. In that shining realm, we sit together for a while. Then he carries me down, into shadows again, and home.

Like Mama, my husband, Wendell, did not like me to talk about Daddy's suicide, either.

"I try to leave violence at the office," he'd tell me. "I can't come home to yet another grim tale, Rose."

By "the office," he meant the F.B.I. building in Washington, D.C. Wendell worked in Fingerprints for thirty-odd years. He never could rid his nails of the residue collected there like coal-mine grime, like furnace soot. Months would pass. I'd keep my silence. Memory shoved up under my heart, pressing against my ribs, shooting pain down my leg, up my back to my shoulder blades, sometimes straight to my head. Migraines, I called those attacks, when really the cause was Daddy poised on my brain like the ledge off which he'd jumped. If it was a weekend, Wendell would sit beside me on the bed in our darkened room, our boys banished to the park or the movies or a neighbor's apartment, and he'd lay cool washcloths over my throbbing eyes. So long as the pain was in my body, Wendell nursed me with sweet patience. But let me call out to my father in the middle of the night, and Wendell would shake me awake, his voice rough and insistent: "That's enough now, Rose. You're having a nightmare." He said it as if I'd burned dinner or lost my keys. As if he were pointing out some lapse on my part. Some failure. "It's Daddy," I'd say, locked on his image there by the bureau, there by the clothes hamper, now there by the closet door. Wendell would snap on the light. "Don't go stirring up morbid memories," he'd say. "Stop dwelling in the past." Well, what did that mean, after all—"dwelling in the past"—but being at home in your own life? And I wasn't stirring up a thing. That day comes back to me all on its own, like weather, like the sunny day it was, June 5, 1923. Sometimes I wonder what would have happened if it had rained, and we hadn't driven for three hours, my parents and me, into the Blue Ridge Mountains and parked behind the train station where John Brown let that conductor through who sent the troops right back to kill him. What if we had stayed in our farmhouse on Winchester Grade Road and played checkers like we did on dreary days when the rain pelted the tin roof and kerosene lamps burned in every room? It is hard to think that suicide is an urge that comes on you like a passing itch, nothing major, and if you leave it alone, it will give up and stop pestering you by the time you're ready for bed. Hard to think that, but even harder to believe that death had such an urgent claim on someone who wore happiness like a custom-made suit. John Temple—he was all strut and swagger; you'd have thought they'd have to drag him off this earth, not that he'd decide to leave it at the age of thirty-one.

If he wasn't a happy man, I've often thought, who is?

Well, it strikes me now that Karl is. He's out in the backyard, working in a garden better than any I would have imagined. He never gardened when he was married to Florence. I didn't know he had any feeling for it at all. But here he is, hands bare—no gloves—his fingers plunged into the earth, bringing up soil and slugs and worms thick as his thumb. He likes the dirt, this son I always counted fussy. I used to think that being manly meant you had to lunge and charge, careen, through life. That's Justin to the nth, but still he's squeamish. Once his son, Zach, gashed his arm and Justin paled at the blood, I was witness, he could hardly stand to clean the cut and bandage it. Whereas Karl could be a doctor, that's how good he is with pain.

You learn these things over the years. Your children start out as dreams. Gradually a family wakes up to itself, and I have woken up to Karl this morning. Yes.

He's planting petunias. I sit down beside him in the webbed lawn chair, and I say, as if it were ordinary conversation, "When I was five years old, I saw my father jump off a bridge in Harpers Ferry." I have never shared this with anyone, you see, except Wendell and then he'd always put me off. As soon as the words are out, I understand how heavy they'd become inside me all these silent years.

Karl puts down his flowers. He regards me soberly. "You never told me," he says.

"I thought it would give you nightmares."

He looks at his dirt-encrusted hands. "Truth is always a comfort," he says.

I believe that. I say, "I would like to tell you about it now, Karl, except this is a happy occasion, the wedding and all, and—"

"I would be disappointed if you didn't, Mother."

So I describe to him how on that morning, almost two months after I'd climbed that tree to comfort my father, Daddy and Mama packed the picnic basket with hard-boiled eggs, ham sandwiches, pickles and strawberries from the patch by the front door. Daddy gathered up the newspaper and lay it across the food, folded the quilt from my bed and gave it to me to carry. She was in charge of the mesh sack into which she'd put bug-bite ointment, a rubber ball, a deck of cards, her needlepoint project, and three visors we could use if the sun began to bother our eyes. At 7:00 A.M. we got into our Ford. We sat three abreast, me by the window, and rode from one mountain range to another. It was hard to believe that the earth had flat places on it, that there was anything but ascent and descent, that balance came easy anywhere in the world. We braced ourselves against the jostling. I pressed my feet up against the dashboard. Mama held onto Daddy's sleeve and mine. He wedged his shoulder into the corner made by the seat and the door. I told Karl how Daddy and Mama talked to each other most of the way, and I liked how their voices sounded that morning, even though sometimes at home their talk shut me out and I was lonely in their midst. Maybe that came from being an only child. Or maybe my father's unhappiness was in our house all along, living under his words like fish beneath the water's surface. Maybe Mama was right: He put up a good front, and the fire blight was not the beginning of his troubles at all. I do admit that sometimes the sound of them talking to each other at home encircled them like an electrified fence: "Keep out," it said. "Dangerous to children."

But not that morning, not in that car. Maybe because we were all pressed up against each other, connected one to the other like one body almost. I don't know.

"Perhaps you sensed the peace he craved," Karl says softly. "Perhaps you understood that he was close to it now." He is sifting peat moss through his fingers. "Children can be very intuitive, you know."

He has that faraway look he used to get as a boy. Then a small smile works its way through his features, like a swimmer fighting the undertow. "I would like you to continue, Mother," he says. "If you would."

Which I do. I slide back into 1923 like it was on the other side of Karl's fence and I just need to pass through that place where he's taken down two pickets in need of repair.

When we put on the visors, my mother said, "We look like card sharks. Who's for gin rummy?"

She was fishing in the mesh bag for the deck of cards while I helped my father spread the quilt on the grass. Up and down the riverbank, I saw sets of parents and children readying their own picnics. No matter that behind us lay the town of a bloody Civil War battle and several murderous floods, and in front of us the river twisted over sharp rocks and storm-felled trees, their roots upended like claws sticking out of the water.

Mama said, "Here's your hand, John."

On my knees I watched him play.

"Rosie," Daddy said. That was his name for me, and I never allowed anyone, not even Wendell, to use it. "Rosie, you are the best luck this small-time gambler ever had." He rubbed my elbow like I was one of those amulets betting people carry in their pockets and he had everything he owned on this game. He had a look in his eyes that said, "I need magic, Rosie. I need good fortune bad."

I smiled hard. I held my breath and clenched my fingers and toes and made a low growling sound in my throat for him, but Mama called "Gin!" the third time she picked a card from the pile and Daddy lost his nickel and his grin and his good posture all at once.

Mama said, "Now, John, it's just a game," and reached out to tweak him. But he flinched, stood up like a bee was after him, walked off huffy and shamed. I watched him get smaller and smaller until he was just a slash of blue—he had worn blue overalls. I watched him move past where the last clump of people sat, down to the place where the bridge pilings were. From where I was, they looked like toothpicks. The bridge that arched over Mama and me looked like it was holding itself aloft, floating, not attached to anything.

Mama said, "Well, Rose, let's eat our lunch."

She said it strange, as if there were only the two of us.

"When Daddy comes back," I insisted.

But she was taking the food out of the basket, placing it on the blanket. She was holding her head in an angle of reproach, towards me, or Daddy, I couldn't be sure which.

I wanted to run over the grass to where he was and lead him back. I scanned every inch from the blanket to the pilings to the last family in sight. But I couldn't locate that blue form anywhere.

Right then I realized others were searching, too. Or at least they seemed to be. Heads craned all along the grass. Hand after hand pointed upward, and voices rose in a single web of sound, a hummed "ooooohhhhh" that lifted level to the bridge and hovered there like a net in the fierce light of that distant afternoon.

"Mama," I said, "what—"

And then we saw him: too far to make out his features, too near to mistake him for any other man. My father, Daddy, John Temple, swinging a second leg over the railing and stepping off into the air, easy as if the ground were still beneath his feet, falling through the bright air like a bird zooming to earth. What I mean is, something about him seemed to be at home in flight, comfortable in his sudden descent, a winged creature's acrobatics, not a man's last plummet. I felt sure my father would loop up right before impact, soar to the bridge, win everybody's dazed applause.

But Mama's scream was no cheer. Shriek, wail, cry of terror—I thought my head would burst from the sound of it. I had never heard a person make a noise like that, and haven't since.

He glanced off rock, Daddy did, sank into the water's foam and I never saw him again.

The rest of the day drowned with him. I have no recollection of what we did, who took us home. I'm blank on everything up until the moment, four days later, his coffin was lowered into the earth, rain tapping like a child's knuckles on the wood, he not answering the little knocks—no, my daddy deaf to all appeals now, gone down into the final quiet, gone down now, gone.

While I talk, Karl has been separating a carton of white petunias into six separate plants. Tenderly he tugs at the fragile roots, that mass of tangled threads binding the flowers together in their common ground. One by one, he sets the severed flowers on the grass, one by one he plants them in the loamy bed he's prepared with his hands. The blooms wilt from the shock. Stems buckle. He feeds each water, mulches at their feet. They'll revive, I know. Each one will spring back to life in hours. Not my daddy. For the first time, I let myself cry in front of a son of mine. Karl takes me in his earth-stained arms, pats me on the head like I was the child instead of him.

"There's more," I tell him. He gives me a hand-kerchief from his overalls pocket. "There's more."

After Daddy died, Mama joined up with the Faith Evangelical Choir of the Daughters of Zion Pentacostal Church. She practiced her hymns around the house like other ladies hummed "My Blue Heaven." Elsie Stitt, the first soprano, worked as a masseuse at the Lodge. She told Mama she could get her a job there, too, but first Mama had to be trained. We still had the house, but the orchard was up for sale, and Mama needed a way to earn us money. For weeks, Elsie would come home with Mama after choir practice and give her lessons on massage. This was after I'd been put to bed, but one night I couldn't sleep and padded into the parlor from my room upstairs, Mama was lying on the braided rug with nothing but a towel over her privates and Elsie was rubbing oil into Mama's legs.

I said from the doorway, "If my daddy were here, you wouldn't do this."

Mama made a noise like barking. She bolted up and the towel dropped away. Lamplight fell on her oil-shined flesh and she looked for all the world like a stranded seal. "Well, your daddy is dead!" she rasped. "And you know what he left me to raise you with? Eight hundred dollars in debts and a lapsed life insurance policy, that's what!"

She was crying now. I wanted to give her back her towel, but Elsie Stitt retrieved it first and handed it to Mama and I ran upstairs to do my own crying in that pillow where I poured out my nightly grief.

I never said another word to Mama about her massage work, but I knew she didn't like it any more than I did. She'd say things like, "The body is merely the soul's temporary lodging, Rose." Yet she spent all day attending to the flesh she now dismissed. She let herself go. She quit making herself pretty, let her hair get stringy, her smooth skin become puckered and lined like a web, like the inside of an orange peel. This continued for nearly two years. Imagine.

Then she got herself a boyfriend. Mr. Homer Simpson, a just-widowed traveling salesman from Akron, Ohio, who passed through Berkeley Springs on business and decided to have himself a treatment at the

Lodge. Homer Simpson looked very much like W. C. Fields. I used to imagine him cuddling up to Mama and whispering "my little chickadee" into her ear. He started courting her immediately. That very first night he bought her dinner in the dining room, and she came home with eight boxes of wood-handled steak knives (that was his line) and color in her cheeks I hadn't seen since before Daddy died. You'd have thought Homer had given her underwear, the way she blushed showing me that cutlery. Three weeks later he moved himself down to Berkeley Springs and rented a room in a boarding house. Mama dropped out of the choir, started using a curling iron and gave herself facials every night from a concoction of eggs and lemons and mud she dug up from a place under the downspout by the back door.

I couldn't say which I preferred, religion or romance. Both of them made her strange.

I still remember how things were when my father was still alive. Begonias blooming on the windowsills. Starched sheets. Lattice-topped fruit pies cooling on a rack in the kitchen.

"You don't make pies anymore," I told her once.

She said, "All the pies in the world won't bring John Temple back to us."

As if that was my notion. I was the one who was missing her care. But she was gone a lot, first with choir and then with Homer. She never married Homer. They "kept company" until she died. "We're in no rush," she'd say when people asked, which, as you can imagine, they did. "We're taking our time." What I think now is she never got over seeing herself as Mrs. John Temple, so marrying Homer was not a real possibility for her. This is what I think, although we never did discuss it. This theory comes from losing a husband myself and hearing people call me "widow" when I know I'm as married as ever, even if Wendell has "gone to his reward," as they put it.

I don't know where anyone goes when they die. I don't know where Daddy is, or Mama, or Wendell. Unlike my father, Wendell left me insurance money, and after his death years ago, I placed a call to Elton Howard, a realtor in Berkeley Springs. I had been reading the classifieds under MOUNTAIN PROPERTY FOR SALE, which I have done daily for almost forty years, since I married Wendell Fry, left West Virginia and came to live in an apartment building on upper Connecticut Avenue in Washington, D.C. Wendell never wanted a house, said apartment living suited him fine. He said he couldn't be bothered with upkeep. But I have always missed the sense of roaming I had as a girl. All my life I have wanted land. Flowers that would put the National Arboretum to shame. My daddy was a gardener. I can close my eyes and smell the soil he's just upturned, see the startled worms burrowing back into the earth's dark depths. I have plotted out entire yards in my head: how I'd plant the azaleas; where I'd put the clumps of daffodils and tulips, the impatiens. I'd have lots of impatiens, pink and white and that blood red they have, blooming in the shade my cherry and magnolia trees would make. Once I figured out a whole Japanese garden, stone river and all, hyacinths sprouting along the edge of the imaginary water.

"My name is Rose Fry," I said to Elton Howard, "and I am interested in buying a house."

What did I have in mind to spend? he said.

I told him.

"Mrs. Fry—I take it it's missus—that wouldn't buy you more than a barn."

Five years ago I let that stop me, thanked him, had myself a good cry and walked awhile outside, until the traffic din and bus fumes drove me in again. But last night, in my dream, I placed that call a second time. "I'd like to see what you have," I told Mr. Howard, and then I was there, in Berkeley Springs, buying myself two stories of weathered wood and windows taller than Wendell was, over six foot, even at the end.

In my dream, I have acres, some still wild, some cultivated just the way my father had, when life's sweetness counted more for him than its pain. I look out over the Cacapon River. On the opposite bank, fluted rock cliffs rise like a tabernacle built right into the earth. In the morning, I walk up to the pasture, and sun polishes everything—sky, mountains, river, grass, cliffs, even the faded-gray barn siding itself—to such a sheen that it appears the world as I know it is just a thick layer of brightness that could, at any moment, give way like an eggshell or a crust of ice or a lightbulb's fragile glass casing. A whole other world would then reveal itself to me.

I contemplate this awhile. Then I walk back to the barn. Begonias bloom in the window, pies cool on the sill. Between two maples, starched sheets flap like

[39]

sails on the clothesline. I take one down and spread it on the grass.

"It's time for our game!" I call. In the doorway to the barn, he appears—my father, Daddy, John Temple—riffling a deck of playing cards, wearing his gambler's grin. "Get ready, Rosie, my luck's come back!" He strides towards me, into the dazzle, and I swear I'll let him win as many hands as he can play.

Karl says, "You were very brave to remember this, Mother."

He sees that I'm finished.

I am weak, out of breath. You would think I'd just required some hard labor, some task requiring all my strength. My son offers me his hand. He helps me rise. Brave?

"Well," I say, "thank you, dear."

I never knew memory took courage; but now that he's said it, I can see that it's so.

I leave him in the garden and walk back to the house. I can't see the cracks in the stucco or the chipped blue paint with old yellow bleeding through. The sun washes out the flaws and smoothes the walls and blends the colors together. Puts me in mind of a bird's egg, the way it looks so delicate and smooth in the morning light.

Karl used to bring home birds' eggs from his nature walks in the neighborhood. He'd go off on a Saturday with that Easter basket he'd saved one year after he'd eaten the jelly beans and marshmallow bunnies, and he'd come back with his "finds," as he called them. Tiny eggs, tattered nests, stones he'd polish until they'd pass for jewels, leaves he'd paste into a picture album like girls press orchids between the pages of books.

"He's fifteen years old," Wendell would say. "When is he going to get interested in manly pursuits?" As if Wendell were. As if he'd ever played ball or gone hunting or come home from school with bloody noses and torn shirts himself. Never. I pointed that out to him: "He's quiet like you are, Wendell; he likes to be by himself." But he'd turn on me: "If my sons can't do better in life than their father, I'd as soon never had children at all." Then his face would darken, like a shade had been pulled down inside and he was closed off to me. The truth is, Wendell did not much care for himself. Oh, he put on a show, and some people even found him conceited. The way he bragged about the Bureau, the fuss he made about his clothing being pressed, not a piece of lint allowed, shoes brushed every morning whether they needed it or not. When he reprimanded the boys, he always said, "I am your father!" like that amounted to something major in his eyes, like he thought himself lordly. Truth was, he didn't. Anything he saw in Karl or Justin that reminded Wendell of himself, he took as trouble. Which, you can see, is trouble itself.

Wendell, I think as I reach the back door, *you can stop worrying about Karl. He may still be quiet, but he's really not like you at all.*

Charlotte's taken Mary to the dentist this morning, and once inside, I look the house over like I'm a prospective buyer. I have always played that game with myself, in every house I ever visited. What if I lived here? What if this were mine? It's not envy I feel—I don't begrudge anyone their own home—it's just been my way of having one myself. Of course, the apartment is a home, I've made it one, but always this longing for porches and yards and steps you climb. Once Wendell said, "Just because you had your childhood in a house, Rose, doesn't mean it's the best way to live." But I venture to say that for me it is.

It comes to me now that Fry's Lodge reminds me of our farmhouse. As soon as I walked in here yesterday, I was comfortable. Which was strange, seeing how I've had such doubts about Karl, about the way he'd come down here in the first place, with no job and no trade and not a soul he could call friend, and the next thing I know he's married to Charlotte and gone into business, both of them in hock up to their ears. Lonely people make bad decisions. That was my view, and seeing this place from the outside didn't change my mind one iota. Yet soon as I stepped over the threshold, a pleasure came over me deep as a bride's who's been carried into a new life by her groom. I tried to keep my guard up, but this house is the closest thing to home I've known since a girl, and it's Charlotte who's made it so nice.

Take the kitchen here, the way she's fixed it up. Over the linoleum is a braided rug, covers the whole floor mostly, and the walls are done up in this paper looks just like the patchwork quilts the ladies stitched in Berkeley Springs. She's painted the cupboards honey-gold, and copper pots hang from those racks that look like bonnets. Creeping figs on the plant stand beside the door, and above the sink a glass shelf spanning the window holds African violets and those begonias I have always loved. You have to pinch the blooms in time to keep them flowering, but they're worth the upkeep. Mama had the best luck with begonias. I learned from her. On the table there's a nice clean cloth and cloth napkins set out for supper. In the middle of the table, a wooden lazy Susan holds salt and pepper, a sugar bowl, paper napkins in a holder each side of which looks like a pear, and a jar of Smucker's orange marmalade. You know people live here. You know they enjoy sitting together here. Justin would say, "You know what you want to know and you palm it off as the truth." I'd tell him, "A boy who distorts everything ought to be addressing himself."

Look. In their room, they have a four-poster bed. You hear Miami Beach, you think water beds and saunas, newfangled comforts dragged into the home. Not here. Mama and Daddy didn't have a four-poster, but they did have an heirloom spread just like the one Karl and Charlotte have. Wedding ring pattern. Mama gave it to me when I married Wendell (it had been stored away for years, with mostly everything else that Mama associated with "John's time," and she'd bought a polyester quilt, Springtime Garden pattern, at J. C. Penney to replace it). We used it until Justin was fourteen years old and burned a hole in it, right in the center, with a cigarette. What he was doing in our room I never could determine. Wendell said, "He went in there to destroy something, and he did." I don't know. The burn went through the thermal blanket, the top sheet, and left a brown stain on the bottom sheet as well. We were lucky everything didn't go up in flames. I darned the hole, but it still looked marred, plus every time it caught Wendell's eye, his pressure shot up. So I folded it up like Mama had done and packed it in a cardboard box full of mothballs and slid it under the bed, where it still rests today. To see its twin in Karl and Charlotte's room! It's a gift. As if Daddy jumping off a cliff and Mama getting rid of all the things that reminded her of him (Did she want to get rid of me like that? Did I bring her back to Daddy every time she saw my face?) and Justin ruining what I'd finally retrieved—well, it's as if loss and disappointment aren't the bottom line, you see, it's proof again this earth's a friendlier place than it might appear. Imagine what Justin would say to that: "You think life's one big Hallmark greeting card, don't you? Best wishes and congratulations on your new job and happy birthday and get well real soon, don't you? It's all bullshit, you hear me? It's all a scam." Oh, I get a little woozy hearing his voice in my head. I settle myself on the field of white knots just until the dizziness passes, but while I rest I forget where I am. Is this Mama and Daddy's bed? Am I home at last?

I've been here for two days now. It's Thursday morning and I'm having lunch with Diana. When I come down from my bath, Karl's left for the cabins with clean towels and Charlotte's hanging sheets on the backyard line. I had watched her from the window by the tub—the wind puffed out the sheets like sails, you'd have thought for a minute the house were a ship, the ground not ground at all but water, this seeming stillness voyage.

I felt it so strong, waves rose in the bathtub, I could have sworn they broke on my thighs.

You'd think I traded in my common sense since I've been down here, all the notions I've been getting. Next thing you know, ghosts will pop up and I won't even be fazed.

To be honest, I've given that a thought or two. At home I listen to this psychic on the radio who gets people together with their dead relations right on the air. They carry on the same as when all of them were living. "Listen, Fred," one lady told her deceased husband, "you left me with bills I didn't know we had. That loan from Master Charge and eighty-six dollars at Hecht's for a brand-new fishing rod when you said we couldn't afford to fix the roof until next year, and—" "Now, Sylvia"—you could hear all the years of squabbling in his voice, only the real Fred could have said her name like that—"the roof would have run in the hundreds. You don't have to make me sound like I chose the fishing rod over the roof. You don't have to make me sound like a liar and a spendthrift on the radio, Sylvia. Just because I'm dead, that don't give you license to make me out a nitwit."

Life keeps on being ordinary, no matter what you try.

In the parlor, Mary's singing. By singing, I mean her own off-key word-bent version of "Rock of Ages," which she's picked up on some gospel music station. I know gospel, all right. Mama taught me that.

There's Diana's horn. My timing's been just right. "Mary, she's here!" I holler, but how can my lonely voice compete with God's entire hallelujah chorus? The music's gone inside her, entered her bones—her body and the music are one thing now. She sways and dips like a girl who's taken dancing lessons for years, when of course she's normally clumsy and stiff in her movements. And her pitch has improved some, the tune's not so mangled now. Puts me in mind of a radio station coming in clearer and clearer the more you jiggle the knob. Well. Who knows what gets woken up when in a person? Maybe Mary's just been asleep more than most, having a long dream, and now she's roused to her true life. It could happen. Of course, it isn't scientific. Of course, Charlotte's had her to specialists and all. Oh, I know. She is what she's always been, a poor girl with half a brain, but you wouldn't come to that if you were witness now instead of me. I leave her undisturbed in her joy.

Diana's parked her bright red car on the gravel next to Karl's jeep and she's coming towards me over the hot stones. The air's turned thick as beveled window glass and though I can recognize her beauty twenty feet away, still she looks the smallest bit distorted to me. Like all the parts of her don't quite fit together. Not until we're square on top of each other does she appear entirely normal, and even then I have to squint some to get her right. What with rain, snow, fog, when there isn't humidity to deal with, it's amazing we ever see another person clear, as they really are, at all. Perhaps we never do. Think on that. "Well, give this old lady a hug and a kiss!" I screech. Sound like a parrot, but at my age vanity takes a back seat to most all else. When we embrace, I smell her youth powerful as good perfume.

"Grandma," she says, "that is a beautiful hat!"

I'm wearing the white straw Wendell brought me the time he went to the 23rd Annual Convention of Law Enforcement Professionals in Atlantic City. This was 1959, before they turned it into a gambling town. The hat's got a wide pink sash that trails down your back. Wendell usually brought me practical gifts: egg beaters, bedroom slippers, dish-towel calendars. When he gave me that hat, I said, "My, my, what is repsonsible for this impetuous gesture?" I was giddy from the pleasure of it, prancing around the kitchen like I was Scarlett O'Hara being courted by Rhett.

"To be truthful," Wendell said, because candor was what he valued over sentiment, "the man I shared a room with had bought it for his wife, but they'd had a spat over the phone and he said I should take it or he'd throw it away. So I did. Actually, I was afraid you'd think it silly."

That cut short my dance, but I managed to hold on to some of the pleasure of the gift. After all, half of it was for the hat, half for the hope that Wendell had chosen it for me; I still had the first part. This is a skill that comes from losing a parent, or a son, or anything you love: You learn to pull into yourself what's left you, to count it dear; at least you do this if you're smart.

I pivot around so Diana can admire me properly, from all angles. Coming to rest, I tell her, "I'm so glad you like it. When I was getting dressed, I realized I've yet to take a walk on the beach since my arrival and I hoped I'd get to do that with you, dear."

This is what makes Karl's cabins the bargains they are: You have to walk or ride nine blocks and cross a highway before you get to the ocean. Still, even from the main house you can smell the salt and at night I swear the tide tugs at your dreams. I've become like sea myself, time turned to water, past and present mingled now, not separated into two countries, each with their own borders and laws and language. Life's turned fluid, deep in unexpected places.

"You mean they haven't taken you swimming yet?" Diana says. She rolls her eyes at the thought of it. "They get so caught up with running this place, they forget what it's for. I don't think my father even has a bathing suit."

I don't condone her criticism, I know how those two can wound each other, yet it's nice to see her spunk. I think she gets a share of it from me. Before Karl and Florence divorced, and they lived nearby, and I saw Diana weekly or so, I would think: *If I had a girl-child, it would be like this—my body's clock run backwards, my aging features young again in her child face.* Florence hated how Diana looked more like me than even Karl or Justin did, and nothing like the Langleys at all. You would have thought my genes had rested up in Karl for twenty-odd years, then worked double-time once Diana was conceived. Often I'd get the urge to rush over to their house—they had a nice Cape Cod in Arlington, even if the planes did make a racket taking off and landing so near to them—I'd want to go right over and say, "Florence, Karl, I'm sorry but she's mine. You can see it easily, I'm sure. You've been more than generous, caring for her these years. But a true parent needs her true child, and vice versa. Experts agree on this, you can find whole books that take my side. You can argue as much as you want, but as of today Diana Fry is coming home with me." Imagine having such an idea about your own son's daughter. Of course, the daydream would pass, drift off like so much fluff. But that's how seeds travel, don't they; floating away weightless from one place to put down somewhere else, sprouting roots that turn out tougher than rock if you try to yank them out of the ground.

When Florence decided to move down here with Diana, and Karl put up so little fuss, guilty and glum as he was at the time, I knew I'd lost my last chance to have her, this child with my face and good posture and the same habit I have of chewing the inside of my cheek when I'm nervous. I chewed my cheek raw the two weeks after they'd gone; I had to go to the doctor for an antibiotic and something to help me sleep. I never let on to Karl how bad my grieving was, but nights I'd howl in my bed like an animal whose lair's been robbed. I lost twelve pounds; my hair fell out in clumps; I kept getting cramps in my toes so bad I could hardly walk, let alone get on a plane or bus bound for Miami to make a fool of myself, which I have been known to do in my life more times than I care to remember. Then the pain was gone; in its place one more emptiness: Daddy, Mama, Wendell, Diana, Justin—in his way—all of them gone from me like parts of my body I have had to learn to live without. Agnes Shaw, in my building, she has lost a kidney, a breast, half her heart is plastic and now an eye is failing: We get whittled down in different ways is all.

Standing beside Diana, I see Karl's little girl, the one I mothered in my heart, furled like a baby asleep in her womanly flesh. Oh, I am moved to such tenderness! You might think I'd put this child up for adoption years ago and here I was reclaiming her, that's how choked up and shaky I suddenly am.

At a red light, Diana turns from the wheel to catch me dabbing at my eyes. "I suppose you think I'm a horrible person," she says, "that I didn't want to talk to Mary."

The child had stood on the porch and called for Diana—"Di! Di! Di!"—but my granddaughter didn't budge from her car. Finally, I went to Mary myself, told her I'd bring her a treat from the restaurant. This quieted her some, though I could see she had a sadness in the smile she gave me. Yet hadn't I had the same feelings about Mary before I'd spent these days in Karl's house? Didn't I feel squeamish myself about her condition?

And she is the one being fathered by the man who'd left his other home, when Diana was a child, then gone to live in this second family instead. I know what Diana's borne, though it was clear to me when they married that Karl and Florence would never make each other happy, would never be for one another that buffer against the world's travails, that raft in white water.

"You know your grandma's no holier-than-thou type," I say.

"Then how come you're crying?"

I reach over to smooth her golden hair, mussed up by the car's breeze. "I'm remembering you in diapers, the time you—"

But she pulls away. "C'mon, Grandma." She shifts into drive. "I'm grown."

We tear out of the intersection like Diana was racing out of the past itself.

I say, "We had sweet times together."

She doesn't look at me, but her hand crosses the space between us and rests a moment on my knee. She sniffs a few times. She is a beauty, that girl; she could do TV commercials.

"Sinuses," she says, lest I misread.

"Oh yes. This humidity. Bad as we have at home. I bet you don't remember Washington summers. D.C. was built on a swamp, you know. Most people aren't aware of that."

I can tell she's willing to remember some with me now, lean back a decade and browse, as it were, same as if we were in an antique shop or a museum. So what if we can't take home a Rembrandt or a Louis XIV chair, as long as we can linger a bit over something lovely?

At the Reef we have a table right up by a windowed wall. The beach is no more than twenty feet from us.

"There's nothing like a body of water," I say, "to calm a person down."

"It pales," Diana says.

She's not eating her shrimp salad. She's looking through the wide expanse of glass out to the Atlantic, but it doesn't seem to soothe her much. And she's chewing her cheek, a dead giveaway from one Fry to another that things are less settled than they seem.

I wade in. "Everybody's nervous getting married, Diana."

She stares at me as if I've read her mind. People are so used to being ignored, you just pay someone a little heed and they're convinced you've got ESP powers.

I go on: "Nervous is a small word for it. Scared to death. Terrified. Some get hives, vomiting, fever—you'd think they'd been struck down by plague."

"I'm not scared of Sam," she says. "I love Sam."

"Of course you do. But I know the things going through your mind. He might leave you someday, or die, or just turn quiet on you, brooding on the unnamed disappointment you'll spend your life trying to overcome. He might realize after a year or two that you reminded him all along of his Aunt So-and-so, who he never could stomach, or his fourth-grade teacher who gave him detention for ten days when he hadn't done a thing wrong, or the girl who jilted him when he was fifteen years old and in love for the first time. Or all of those things might be true on *your* end, and *Sam* will be the one bewildered and grieved. Everybody worries that things like this will happen. Then again, some people can't stand the happiness of love—they feel themselves getting bigger and bigger, like they were being pumped full of helium, and any minute might lift off the earth, separated from everything familiar, lost in the clouds forever. People have these feelings, Diana. Nobody likes change, nobody likes—".

"I want to marry Sam," she says. "I really didn't expect you to be giving me doubts I don't have."

She's all tensed up, warding me off. That fern plant hanging from the ceiling could be my granddaughter's ragged nerves; you know how the fronds look like a current's passing through them, feeding them constant tiny shocks.

"Of course you want to marry Sam. What I meant was, if you could get your fears on the table and out of your system, the way you do a nightmare you tell someone about, you'd be able to feel your confidence again. You got to get the other out, though, else it's a bone in your throat."

That last remark comes to me while checking through my filet of flounder. Wendell always picked his fish apart and I inherited the habit.

She's holding herself, shivering.

"Let's walk on the beach awhile," I say. "I could use a little sun, couldn't you? All this air-conditioning gives a person a chill."

In the bright heat, I wait for Diana to talk. But she's pulled into herself as completely as any of the sea creatures living in the conch shells you find on the sand. How many times have I seen that look on Justin's face, the look that says *I am beyond your care.*

Justin wakes me up at 4:00 A.M. In a dream, I mean. Or something like a dream. He is in this room is all I know. He walks in and slumps in that rocker like he's just finished a whole night of shooting baskets, which he used to do as a boy. Hours on that court, even after dark when all the other boys had gone home, he'd be bounding alone over the darkened asphalt, aiming for the hoop he saw same as if the sun were out.

I sit up in bed. "Justin? Are you sick? Is something wrong?"

One afternoon when he was in second grade, he didn't come home for lunch like he should. Here I'd just brought him through a week of strep throat and fever, and worrying that it would go to his heart (Isn't strep the one that can go to your heart?) and now I'm facing hit-and-run or kidnapping or—well, you can imagine the places my mind was traveling. Ever since Karl had been in the first grade, lunchtime had been the same. At eleven-thirty, I'd set up the bridge table in the parlor, put on a cloth, and make the boys their sandwiches. Boiled ham was their favorite, or sometimes I'd fix soup. Justin was partial to Campbell's tomato soup with some Oysterette crackers mixed in. So I'd have lunch all fixed, and when they came in at noon, we'd be all ready to watch the stories. "Search for Tomorrow" and "The Guiding Light," we watched them religiously, first me and Karl and Justin, then just me and Justin when Karl was off in junior high and eating in the cafeteria. By twelve-thirty and still no sign of my youngest son, I was so nervous I was nearly asleep. This is what happens to me when I'm scared. I don't get jumpy like some, I go still. Everything inside me loses power. I swear my blood itself slows down. But I managed to put on my shoes and sweater and walk the seven blocks to Grover Cleveland Elementary School. I was in a trance, that's how sleepy I was. I must have looked brainwashed, hypnotized, walking into that empty building and right into the principal's office and saying to the

[54]

secretary there, "Something terrible has happened to my son, Justin Fry."

"You mean on the second-grade picnic," she said, rising up in alarm from behind her Remington. "An accident on the bus?" I sank down on the wooden bench under the big clock. "I didn't know about any picnic, I—"

"But Mrs. Fry," she said, "your boy called you this morning, right from this phone, came to get your permission since he'd been out sick last week. I heard him talk to you, Mrs. Fry, with my own ears."

I said, "Not to me," suffering that wave of disloyalty that sweeps through you when you disclaim kin. "I was over at the church all morning, working on the centerpieces for the Youth Group dinner this coming weekend."

Just then we heard a rumble in the schoolyard. The bus wheels whipped up dust like a flurry of chickens under attack. Mustering up outrage, I marched outside and watched the children disembark. Justin one of the last to come through the door. I'm standing there like a policeman, but do you think he's quaking or shamed at the sight of me? No. Justin Fry, grinning for all he's worth, fingers raised above his head in a V-for-Victory sign, salutes, enters that schoolyard like a regular hero just back from the war.

Right then I knew: He was outside my mothering. When I was a girl, my daddy brought me a magnet and I loved to sit down with a bunch of nails and place them in a circle. Then I'd put the magnet in the middle and watch the nails move into the center. I'd make the circle bigger and bigger, looking for the point where the magnet didn't have a hold on those nails anymore. When I saw Justin get off the bus that day, I saw he hadn't gone off to spite me at all. No, what had happened was graver than that. A child gets out too far, he can feel himself as much an orphan as one whose mama and daddy have truly died. I tried to explain it to Wendell that night, but he wouldn't hear a word of it.

"That boy is going to turn into a juvenile delinquent, Rose, if you keep coming up with theories like that every time he transgresses."

He gave him fifteen whacks with the hairbrush and sent him to bed without his dinner. I couldn't eat a bite of my own. Wendell and I never did see eye to eye on bringing up children.

Now Justin's voice comes from a far distance, not from the body I know I could touch if I moved two feet from footboard to chair.

"I missed you," he says. "I needed to see you before I went."

"Before you went where, Justin?"

I lean as far forward as I can without falling over onto my head, trying to get close to him. Why don't I just get out of bed, if I am so sure of his presence? I can't explain. Something keeps me bound to this mattress, as if it were the world itself, and leaving its support, I'd be pitched into space, rootless, gone from this life.

"And if I don't come back," he says, "I wanted you to know I love you, Mother, I—"

"Now, Justin, you're scaring me!" I want to know exactly—"

But he is gone. Or I wake up. Shivering in the heat—I had to put a cold washcloth on my stomach to get to sleep in the first place, but now I feel as chilled as if winter had overtaken the air. I wait until six-thirty, and then I can't wait any longer. Quietly, so as not to wake Karl and Charlotte, Mary peaceful in her room, I make my way to the kitchen and call Justin. No answer, as I feared. I dial Grace.

"Dear," I say, "it's Rose. I had this dream, you see, and it is still so real to me, I can't—"

"Was it about Justin?" she says, and I know from her voice he's come to her, with his love and his warning and his disappearance.

"Is this a new prank of his?" I say. "Has he figured out a way to terrify people in their sleep as well as in—"

"Rose."

"He says he's going somewhere and he might not come back. Just like that. And I should know he loved me; he wants me to know that. And he looked so tired, Grace, he—"

"He does love you, Rose."

As if that were the important part. As if his whereabouts didn't count for much, his being sick or in danger or confused in his mind not the point.

"He's a grown man," she says. "We both have to remember that. And he's a courageous man."

"How do you mean, courageous? I don't know what you mean by that."

"I just mean that he does what he has to, and sometimes that puts him at risk. To many people, Rose, your son is still a hero."

She is talking in riddles just like his.

"I'm calling from Karl's," I say.

"I know. And will you give everyone my best?"

"Grace, are you worried to death about Justin or not?"

"If he were actually in trouble, would worrying help him?"

I feel my own fear sprouting from my body like tentacles all tangled up in each other, not good for anything except keeping me trapped in their knotted net.

"You give the children kisses for me," I say. "You tell them Grandma will take them to the zoo when she gets home from Cousin Diana's wedding."

"I will, Rose," Grace says. "And Rose: He does love you, dear."

Back in my room, I sit down in the rocking chair and it holds me for a while in its comfort. I will my fear away; I give it the form of a huge chunk of ice and I melt it down with the heat of my concentration. Then I hear my family stirring and I take in the sound of their presences and I say to my absent son: "I love you, too, Justin, wherever you are."

JUSTIN

"What a shock," his mother said when he answered the phone. "You're home."

"No," he said. "Actually, this is a recording of my voice. Would you care to leave a message for me when I return?"

"Do your jokes in a nightclub, Justin, where they'll pay you for rudeness. What I'm calling to ask you is, Are you going to Diana's wedding?"

"Didn't know she was getting married," he said.

"It's hard for me to believe that your own brother wouldn't invite you to—"

"It's hard for you to believe most things about your own family. You are still working so hard at 'Father Knows Best' when actually—"

"Don't insult me, Justin, I am still your mother."

"You haven't always behaved like one," he said, silencing her.

He saw her hand clench the receiver as if she had just been stunned by a slight blow to her ear. He sighed; a rescue disguised as impatience, an offering to her of his own breath.

"I'll give everyone your best," she said, recovered enough to speak.

"Who was it?" Grace said.

She came out of the bedroom wearing Justin's army camouflage jacket as a robe. Justin was never in the army, but he liked the garb, felt comfortable in combat fatigues and boots made for slogging through jungle swamps.

"*La mère*," he answered his ex-wife. "Mrs. Noritake. China, service for eight."

She ignored him, took out four eggs from the small refrigerator in the closet-sized kitchen, cracked each egg hard against the metal bowl, fished out shell fragments with a finger's probe. Justin lay down on the daybed.

"Mrs. Tuesday Night Bingo," he said. "Mrs. 'Family Feud.' "

But Grace was beating the eggs; his words got chewed up in the noise.

He lit a joint. Exhaled smoke rose to the twelve-foot ceiling, disappeared into the carved scrolls and crevices of the molding of this once-elegant building. Now the ceiling was webbed with cracks, the painted-over wallpaper pulled away from the plaster like blistered skin. Last winter, Justin's neighbor upstairs, an exiled Argentine given to fits of bad temper at three A.M., had called the City Health Department to report that Justin was using his fireplace and the smoke was backing up into the Argentine's apartment. The tenants were forbidden to use their marble-fronted fireplaces because the chimney needed work and the landlord, a Mr. Olsen in McLean, refused to do it. When Olsen called Justin to complain about the violation with which he, Olsen, had been slapped, Justin countered: "And what should we do for you when the toilets back up? Piss in the alley?" Olsen hung up. Justin spent the next hour in the Argentine's apartment. "We are being pitted against each other by our common adversary," Justin said in Spanish, "when it's in our interest to cooperate. It's the classic capitalistic model. The man with the resources creates false conflicts among those he exploits in order to keep them from uniting against him and demanding their rights. A feudal strategy. Very effective. For that reason, and also for this"—he dipped a spoon into the pot of paella simmering on the stove—"I propose peace and collaboration." He tasted the savory liquid. *"Muy rico, amigo, muy muy rico."*

They organized a rent strike. Olsen turned off the heat. The Argentine summoned a *Post* reporter to the building—Justin Fry's name made the situation newsworthy—and only after the story appeared in the paper did Olsen relent. He fixed the chimney, and rebuilt the crumbling front steps as well.

In the midst of the protest—when pipes were freezing over and Justin had to wear a ski parka and gloves to sleep, when he had to come to Grace's house to visit the children because he could not have them in his frigid rooms—she asked him, "Why do you stay here? What are you proving? It's a bad neighborhood. Why—"

"It's American. You know me, I'm a sucker for the American way."

"Everybody in America doesn't live with bars on their windows and four locks on their doors. Do they?"

"I'll take the bars on the windows over a locked-up brain, thank you. I lived in that particular penitentiary for a good many years, you may remember. Fry's Prison. Wendell Fry, Warden, otherwise known as 'Dad.' Mother Rose and Brother Karl, trusties. Justin Fry: bad behavior, all privileges suspended, affection denied. I believe I have told you something of my former life? I believe we once were married? I believe you once claimed you understood me, even shared some of my ideas, or do I confuse you with another woman named Grace?"

He was yelling. He had not meant to go that far, get that angry. From the living room doorway, the children had watched him screaming at their mother.

Now she brought out toast and eggs, and mugs of coffee doctored with cinnamon and a pinch of salt. In the corner of the living room that Justin had converted into an eating area, she set their breakfasts on the small wooden table that used to be his desk when they lived together in the rowhouse three blocks from the National Zoo. Sometimes at night they heard hyenas, sometimes elephants trumpeted to them in their sleep. Once Justin had run over a peacock that had escaped its pen and wandered onto Connecticut Avenue. He and Grace had argued that morning, and he was still distraught, did not believe the peacock was real. He had been visited by grander apparitions in his life. By the time he had understood he was not hallucinating, it was too late to stop. He felt the thud rise up his legs, infuse his chest and arms, center in his head, where, for days, it reverberated like a tribal drum. Grace had to clean the feathers off the dented bumper for him. Three days later he had moved out, leaving her with the scarred VW; the children, ages one and three; most of the furniture and a letter which said, in part: "Sweet Grace, I have run out of reasons for staying. Call you in a day or two when I know where I am, geographically speaking."

"Where are you?" Grace said now.

Justin's eyes were sleepy, unfocused, as if they were blind to the room and the woman and the food in their midst. Yet the half smile on his lips, the rise of color in his cheeks, the methodical tapping of his finger on his denimmed knee—all evidence of attention to some interior drama, some script in which he played all parts, directed, viewed from the audience the performances he created.

"I'm thinking about Diana's wedding," he told Grace.

"When did she get married?"

He joined her at the table, speared a forkful of eggs. "She didn't. She's about to." He grinned through his swallow. "Another lucky bastard welcomed into the bosom of the Fry family."

"Your mother called to tell you?"

"To tell me and tell me and tell me."

"I don't—"

He cut her off. "No, you don't; of course you don't. Nor did you grow up at her knee, which means on yours. I never learned to assume the supplicant's position, you see, I—"

"She has never struck me as tyrannical, Justin."

"She's a double agent, baby. Best in the business. Took me years to figure out that lady's scam. All that 'I'm just a girl from the hills of West Virginy' baloney. That's her cover. Eat your eggs, they're getting cold."

"I hate it when you talk like this."

"I would advise you to get a divorce if you hadn't already taken that wise step on your own behalf."

Like figures in a frieze, they sat silent now, stiff with grief: the kind they have learned to handle, biting it off in small pieces, the taste of bile hardly noticeable anymore. Grief, after all, is Grace's profession, her art, her ideology. Doesn't she counsel the dying at the St. Francis Hospice with the same dedication Justin used to bring to anti-war meetings on campuses all over the country? Doesn't she run classes for the bereaved, leading the mourners through the process of loss as Justin used to guide an auditorium of students through the stages of civil disobedience?

He pulled back from the table, his chair settling in a swatch of late morning sunlight. In its warmth, he relaxed, seemed to lose pounds as his anger sank—where? to his toes? into the floor?—and Grace was revived by the sight of his equanimity. She put a record on the stereo: Jean Pierre Rampal. She danced each morning to his improvisational flute, movements she remembered from the ballet classes she had taken as a girl. Plié, eleveé, arabesque: her body bending, rising, arcing; a rush of spins; then repose again. From childhood, Grace had always been disciplined, responsible, had demanded of herself the dedication and exactitude of a ballerina's regimen at the barre. "Dance frees me," she had told Justin when they met. But he had known her to be dependable on sight, steadfast to the core.

Now he watched the woman to whom he'd been married for seven years move her body to the music's sway. In spite of the call from his mother, in spite of discomforts whose sources he had given up trying to trace, he thought he might weep at the sight of this woman, dancing to Rampal in a camouflage jacket, her short black hair a frizzed corona around her small-featured face.

He came up behind her so she would not see his tears and guided her back to bed.

"I was dancing," she said beneath his weight.

"And beautifully," he said, still not letting her look him in the eyes.

He owed his mother for Grace, which was an irony he often fondled. In 1971, Rose had made one of her trips from the respectable regions of Washington, D.C.'s upper northwest, by bus, to DuPont Circle, walking the five blocks to the building he lived in then.

"All those hippies loitering in the streets," she had said. "All those degenerates."

"Those degenerates are my friends."

"Your friends? Don't be foolish. You're an educated man, a professional man; they are bums and derelicts."

"You do recall I was disbarred six months ago?"

"Oh, I'm certain they'll reinstate you, Justin, after the parole period. I'm sure—"

"It doesn't work that way, Mother, and I'm surprised that your husband, alias my father, hasn't educated you more fully. Being"—he had imitated a cowboy drawing his guns—"a law-'n-order man, F.B.I. honcho, no doubt up for a medal for turning in his very own son—"

"To protect you, Justin! So you wouldn't be shot! So the Klan wouldn't lynch you! Did you know the Klan wanted to lynch you? They did!"

"Don't make excuses for him. He turned me in. I was underground. I called up Karl just so you would all know I was alive. He told Wendell where I was, and *voila!* the Feds had me the next day. But perhaps you've heard this little anecdote before, Mother? Why don't you write it up for *Reader's Digest*? 'Life in These United States.' "

"He's dying, Justin."

"They'll give him the medal posthumously."

"I want you to see him."

"I saw enough of him for twenty-seven years."

"I want you to do it for me. He won't even know you, but I need for you to see him, Justin."

He was ready with another rejoinder when he saw her face cave in on itself, all tone vanished, a nerve in her cheek twitching like the last bit of life in her.

"All right," he said. "All right."

The next day, he had stood in the doorway to Wendell's room, Justin's palms pressed to the frame, as if to ground the anger in his hands. Touch his fingers and they would have sparked.

"And who are you?" he had said. A woman sat by the bedside. "Florence Nightingale?"

"Grace Tobias," she said. "I'm the social worker on this floor. I was just leaving." She hung Wendell's chart at the foot of the bed.

"I'm his son," Justin said, as if he owed her that, as if he needed to justify his presence in his dying father's room, as if he were an interloper and she were the legitimate visitor.

"Yes," she said. "I know who you are. I watch the news. I'll be getting out of your—"

"I would rather you stayed."

She had looked at him. "Why is that?"

"We don't get along." He tensed again, voltage coursing through his lanky frame. "Actually, we hate each other."

She approached him, risked shock, lay her hand on his forearm. "Mr. Fry," she whispered. "Your father is in a coma."

For a moment she saw his body yield to that defeat, in the midst of its magnitude she saw his face go slack, then harden again in refusal, in denial. "When he realizes I'm here, he'll come to. He wouldn't give up a chance to get in a few licks."

"We give each other strange gifts," she said.

"We never gave each other a thing."

"Then why are you here?"

Justin had noticed the way her fingers moved to shape the words she spoke, her voice a dulcimer's hushed precision. Nothing glib here. Nothing facile.

"For my mother."

"Then he gave you that," she had said, and left him alone with the dying man.

For twenty minutes, Justin had sat on the chair beside Wendell's bed. Once Justin had looked directly at him—the IVs and the heart-monitor wires attached like strings to a withered puppet—and felt, for an instant, pity that a man's life should end in such exposed helplessness. But then, this particular man was, in fact, his father, and that identification brought forth an entire file, as it were, thorough as an F.B.I. surveillance log. Years of evidence collected and stored and none of it redeeming—for Justin—none of it forgivable, especially that final entry, that last and most definitive betrayal. *All right, Rose, I said I would come. Now you and Karl can resume your noble deathwatch. I have other things to do.*

He had sought out Grace in her office. She was at her desk, writing on a yellow legal pad. On the wall above her head, he took in the bright yellow poster, stick-figure children playing beneath an oversized sunflower, "War Is Not Healthy for Children or Other Living Things" scrawled as if in a child's hand across the bird-strewn sky.

"I would like to talk to you some more," he had said.

She looked up from her work. "We can make an appointment now," she said. "Wednesday mornings, or—"

"Not professionally. As a friend."

"A friend."

"Could we have dinner one night?"

"I'm not sure that would be appropriate."

"I'm not your patient. My father is."

"I suppose—"

"Tonight or tomorrow."

"Tomorrow."

Justin and Grace had dinner the following evening in the hospital cafeteria. She worked the three-to-eleven shift, so it saved time, staying on the premises. He had asked her to take her dishes off the tray, as he was doing. She had asked him why. "Because," he had said, "it makes this more personal." But what was "this"? Was it the pale-green room in which they ate, walls the

[71]

same shade as the faded uniforms doctors and nurses donned in surgery; the green of a plant losing its chlorophyll, leaves hanging somewhere between life and death, losing vibrancy every day? Or was "this" the food served up in this underground crypt, the light harsh fluorescent, the salads wilted, the veal chopped and reformed into mock cutlets, the spinach cooked to the point of green slime puddling on their plates? Standard cafeteria food, vaguely palatable. Was it "this" he hoped to make more desirable by setting the table, so to speak, as if their dinners had arrived on a waiter's tray, china and crystal set before them, making it seem elegant cuisine they'd savor? That was not Justin Fry's style, that was not an ambience in which he would be comfortable. No. "This" was their time together here, this hour—she understood and he saw that she did—and making it "more personal" meant making it domestic: This is our kitchen, here is our supper; would you like a cup of tea? With the gravity of ritual, she had set her dishes before her. They had eaten in ceremonial silence. Over that meal, he would think later, he had married her.

He waited in the lobby until she had finished. He was reading a book about Vietnam by Bernard Fall.

"I've read that," she had said. She had touched the book's cover, brushing her fingertips over its title. "He had a large soul."

He had taken her to his apartment. It was a dingy place in an unrefurbished brick row house. But no fluorescent glare in this home beneath the earth. He gestured to the pillow-laden bed that doubled as sofa and sleeping place. She folded her crocheted shawl into a neat square and set it on the bed's edge. He lit candles all over the room. They rested in groups on tables, floor, windowsills, bookshelves. She watched him move with a lighted taper in his hand as if he were in a church, preparing the altar for Mass. The room shuddered with warm light. He paused in his office to bring her Beaujolais in a juice glass, Brie cheese and crackers on a chipped plate. Then back to the kitchen, returning with three logs in his arms. It was summer.

"A fire?" she had said.

"Last one of the season. Or first. Whatever. I love fires."

And he had rolled newspaper as carefully as a boy scout, placed it under the grate on which he stacked the logs and some kindling from a basket by the fireplace. On the wall above the mantel, a map of Vietnam blazed in reflected light; a bright blue line ran like a vein through the country's burning heart. "VC progress," he had said when she asked him what the line traced. "The progress of a free people in their own land."

He had studied her face for reaction, tested her stamina in the heat of his conviction. Without ambivalence, she undid the buttons of her silk blouse.

Years later, in another apartment, Grace dressed quickly: She had to pick up Zach and Lisa at the day-care center. She had taken the day off to be alone, shut down, but Justin had called the evening before: "I need to see you." When she had arrived at eight in the morning, Justin was sleeping (she had her own key) and he was

[73]

sleeping now as she left. Or feigning sleep, she was not sure which. She had come to accept his subterfuges as she accepted the scar on his left knee.

From the bedroom window, Justin watched Grace get into her white Honda (the VW died the year before) and when she was gone from his sight, he rummaged through the pockets of the pants he had worn yesterday until he found a matchbook on which a phone number was written in red ink. The phone was in the hallway connecting the living room and bedroom, and Justin had turned the narrow corridor into an office: books on one wall, a scaled-down door on legs against the other. This is where he studied. It is where he wrote the articles that appeared from time to time in *Rolling Stone, The Village Voice, The New Republic, The Nation.* It is where he worked on a book he had been assembling for years, an inquiry into his own politicization, an investigation of his own evolution. "An autobiography," Grace had said when he described it to her. "Minus the personal shit," he had said. She had said, "Minus the life, then." This was also where he conducted other, private business which he discussed with no one in any detail. He dialed the number on the matchbook. He heard the receiver lift.

"Sombrero," said Justin to the silent party.

The password was acknowledged; a man said, "The National Aquarium, Saturday at seven."

Justin decoded, wrote down "the Dancing Crab" and replaced the receiver in its cradle. For Saturday: read Wednesday. Back on the daybed, he rolled another joint. Well, it would give him time to get relaxed. The more relaxed he was tomorrow, the better. After two drags, he was nodding off, the half-smoked reefer turning to ash in the clay pot Lisa had made him for his birthday. He shifted to his side and reached out for Grace as if she were still there, as if they were still in bed together, but his hand rammed plaster, he flinched at the hurt. He plummeted into sleep like a man diving off a cliff: his body twitched several times, then quieted; and soon his breathing was calm as a child's, calm as Zach's and Lisa's, whose sleeping forms he had watched for hours on the nights he opened the daybed for them in their father's house.

He woke at 3:00 A.M., the shadows on the wall confirming his intuition that it was the middle of the night. He was too jumpy to fall asleep again. Even as a child, he'd roam the apartment before dawn, a burglar in his own home; opening the refrigerator door with a thief's finesse, remembering not to flush the toilet, memorizing the places where the floorboards creaked and avoiding them as he padded from kitchen to living room, from dining room to bath. Once Wendell "nabbed" him—that was how his father put it, that was his actual language: "Now I've nabbed you good"—and Justin saw the man's face, rigid with anger, his flesh turned glassy hard in the pale bluish wash of the light of the kitchen stove.

"You're out of line," Wendell said, "disturbing the household at this hour. Entirely out of line."

He glared him back to bed, those eyes like lasers on Justin's pajama-shielded back. At the doorway to his room, he faced his father: "I couldn't sleep. Don't I have a right—"

"You have no rights at all," Wendell had said. "You are a child."

Remembering that encounter, Justin felt less disturbed to be awake; as if Wendell's ghost were still assailing him, but without authority now, without power, outrage issuing from Wendell's mouth like a baby's babble, the sound of his own voice rendering him increasingly helpless, so that finally he cowered in a corner of his son's apartment, his ghostly hands raised in defeat, his son's laugh a mockery he wasn't able to endure.

By the time Justin went to the bathroom and searched the refrigerator for something to assuage his predawn hunger—nothing appealed to him—he was past the pleasure of his fantasy, one-upping Wendell in death a quickly dead idea, like the dreams he couldn't remember, swallowed up in that swarm of half-finished thoughts and atrophied images that riddled his mind.

He took off the shirt he slept in, put on a cleaner one, grabbed his wallet, headed out into the moon-glazed street. Although he spent a lot of nights outside like this, walking from his apartment to one of the few taverns still open in this neighborhood, he never got over the loneliness of these hours, the way his footsteps reverberated in the dark, the way in which the distance deepened from one point to another, so that destinations grew remote, even familiar bars a half-dozen day-light blocks away.

"Are you a night person?" Grace had asked him years ago, waking for the fourth morning in a row to find him already gone from their bed.

"No," he had said, "I'm a day person who can't sleep. It's a little like being a man trapped in the body of a woman. Irritating. Extremely. Just one of your basic constitutional fuck-ups."

She had said, "There are cures."

"Oh, Gracie, you're young. Another part of the problem is the refusal to be cured of it, something about the cure being worse than the disease, or the deep-seated suspicion that that may be so."

He was the only one watching the whores. He was waiting for the man who called himself Sombrero. It was Wednesday evening, 7:05. At an outside table, Justin drank a Michelob and watched the whores lounging against the second-floor railing of Sally's Place, next door to the Dancing Crab. A fat woman in a bright yellow dress came out of the front door. In the dusk, her bleached hair looked purple. Justin saw her make the motion of a kiss with her mouth as she approached the patrol car idling in the street. She leaned into the open car window, a white envelope in the hand behind her back. Then the hand, too, entered the car, and returned without the envelope. The driver gunned the engine. As the woman in the tight yellow dress watched the car drive away she wiped her palms on her backside.

"Nice view," Justin said to the waitress. She had brought him a second beer. She looked at him vacantly. He pointed towards Sally's.

"Oh," she said, "I don't pay attention to them."

"They count on that," he said.

She was a thin girl, sallow-skinned, not one of the healthy-looking college students who usually worked here.

She said, "They don't hurt me, far as I can figure."

Justin smiled, said nothing, thought: *That's not very far.* She moved to the next table. Amid the din of smashing mallets, Justin waited for Sombrero.

Sombrero pried up the apron of his seventh crab, removed the shell as easily as if it were a sweater.

"I am a very religious man," he was saying. "In the Hole, I talked with God. I had a visitation from the Holy Spirit—truly—in my cell in Asunción. Have you ever had such an experience?"

"I wouldn't say so, no."

"Believe me, I went in an athiest. I had not been to confession for five years. I consider myself a Marxist, even still, even after the visitation. Many priests in South America, they are Marxists. Jesus was a Marxist, wouldn't you say so?"

Justin added a leg he had picked clean of meat to the pile of shells on the tray between them.

"My theology's weak," he said. "I trust your interpretation."

"Why? What makes you think I am a trustworthy source?"

Justin reached across the table, took hold of the man's muscled forearm, traced the rash of burn scars from wrist to elbow creases with his own finger. "I trust these," he said.

Sombrero laughed. He was a middle-aged man, his ordinary face rutted with strain, his eyes like bruises beneath his brow. But his laugh was unfettered, happy, as if it emitted from a source of well-being protected in him at great cost.

"These?" he said, roaring again, holding his arm as if it were not attached to him at all. "You should see my back. My buttocks. If we weren't in a public place, I would show you their artwork on my behind. Let me tell you, they are artists."

"Picassos," Justin said.

"Sí," said Sombrero, the laugh quieted, the faintest of smiles left on his face. "Picassos."

Justin said, "Shall we talk about our . . . business?"

"I am very curious," Sombrero said, "why you are involved with us. Why you would take this risk."

"Curious or suspicious?"

"I am suspicious of everyone. I am curious about you."

"Would you believe me if I said it was for the money?"

"I would not believe that, no."

"Then it is for all the other reasons."

"Ah." The man called Sombrero relaxed in his chair, closed his eyes as if to sleep for a moment. He sighed. "All the other reasons. *Sí.* That is the best answer, that is the wisest answer." He hoisted himself forward again to the table, shook himself into alertness, a man returning from a dream.

"We want you to go to Miami tomorrow. You will meet an attorney there, Ramon Artigas. He is working on behalf of a number of intellectuals—journalists, professors, doctors—in the cells in Asunción Prison. Our immediate concern is the editor, Samuel Cortez. His health has deteriorated badly, his situation is critical. We are in great demand in Asunción Prison, we intellectuals. Perhaps the government will change the name one day to Asunción Library? Artigas will meet you in the airport at noon. He will wait for you at the United Airlines baggage-claim counter. He has seen your picture, he will know you."

"No more details?"

"Artigas will give you the details. One thing I would suggest: Take warm clothes."

He leaned across the table, squeezed Justin's shoulder with his other hand. *"Gracias,"* Sombrero whispered, as if that was the one secret at the heart of this transaction. *"Gracias, amigo, gracias."*

It was 9:30 when they paid the bill. Justin walked the Latino to his station wagon in the lot behind Sally's Place. On the dashboard, Madonna and child. On the bumper, a sticker promoting a suburban county's soccer league for school children. "My youngest boy is high scorer this season," Sombrero said. He grinned. His teeth flashed in the murky dark. "You also have children, *sí*?"

"*Sí*," Justin said, "I have two children." And he felt in his chest that familiar expansion whenever he referred to Lisa and Zach, a sensation in which the bones and muscles seemed to shift, not without pain, to make room for the presence of his son and daughter, as if he carried their small hearts beside his own, in the shelter of his own body.

Instead of returning to his apartment, he drove to his children's home, to Grace's, the same row house near the zoo where he and Grace had lived together and married and brought each baby from the hospital. The house was filled then with the apparatus of infancy; he suddenly a father whose own father had repudiated him, whose own father had despised him as only a parent can despise a child from whom so much had been desired.

"I'm no good with babies," Justin had told Grace and she had said, "You will never be able to fully love your children until you have grieved for the wounded child in yourself."

"Save it for your clients," he had said. "Spare me your bourgeois Freudian life plan."

Now he stood in the doorway of his children's home.

"They're sound asleep," Grace told him.

"I'll just look in on them," he said. "Kiss them good night. I'm going out of the country for a week or so. Magazine piece. They came through with some money up front, so I don't have to do this one out of my pocket, which, at the moment, is empty."

She searched his eyes. A streetlight rendered them iridescent. "You didn't mention anything about this yesterday," she said.

"If I told you everything, we'd be as good as married again." He turned his face away from her scrutiny. "You have any of that herb tea?"

She made the tea while he went upstairs. In his son's room, Justin found Zach on the upper bunk, a jigsaw puzzle half assembled on the lower bed. A thread of light from the hallway wove through the boy's curls, but Justin could hardly make out the features of his son's face. The father leaned closer, felt the child's breath against his stubbled cheek, but Zach did not stir. "I love you," Justin mouthed. The silent words dropped like coins into a dark well.

In the next room, Lisa slept curled in upon herself, snail to her brother's languid sprawl. She sheltered a doll in the coil her body made, fetus within fetus. The skin of her arm in which her face was hidden shone in a streetlight's wash, and her hair, like Zach's, glowed. He kissed her head, and her body shifted toward his presence, but she, too, remained asleep and Justin deferred to the dream she was having, her lips mumbling a private message into the sheets.

Downstairs, he told Grace, "They're sound asleep," her parental knowledge reclaimed as his own.

They sat outside, in green canvas butterfly chairs, on the small backyard patio. Grace had built it herself with bricks she had salvaged last summer from neighborhood demolition sites. She had lugged home truckloads of fallen walls and chimney ruins. On a bed of sand, the children had helped her lay the vintage stones.

"Where are you going?" she said.

"South."

Moonlight silvered her hair, her face.

He wanted very much to stay with her, in the room next to their children's, all of them breathing the same air again, suffering the dark together.

"I wish you would tell me what this is about," she said.

He shook his head, his lips pursed against a spire of fingers.

"I know it's not an article assignment. Is it?"

He said nothing.

She stood up, a prism of tears on her cheeks. "You better go now. I need to sleep."

He did not suggest he spend the night here, because he understood she had already refused. They had made love many times since their divorce, but never in this house.

"Thank you for the tea," he said, and held her for a moment against him, and left.

On the way home, he thought about the evening several months ago when the young man named Sam Cortez had appeared at Justin's apartment. It was seven o'clock. Justin had had the evening news on while he was making himself supper, canned chili he laced with cayenne pepper, onions, cheese. He stood in the kitchen and ate from the pot. On the screen, Salvadoran soldiers shoved a boy into the back of a truck. When the knock came at Justin's door, he jumped, so wholly had he entered the screen's terror. He had made many trips now to Latin America; he could not hear a car backfire without looking for cover.

"My name is Sam Cortez," the stranger had said. He held out his hand. "My father is a newspaper editor in Asunción, Paraguay, where he is in prison." From his wallet, Sam Cortez took out a picture of himself and Diana Fry, Justin's niece, at the beach. "When Diana told me you were her uncle, I could not get it out of my mind that you could help me. I know of your—work. I know some of your projects."

Justin had stared at Diana's image. He had not seen her for years now. She was one hell of a beautiful girl, that niece of his.

"You're friends?" he said.

Sam had grinned. "We will be married in two months."

"You better be friends, then," Justin had said. "How do you think I can help you?"

They were still standing in the doorway. "If we could talk in private—"

"There's a bar on the corner," Justin had said. "Let me get that TV and grab my billfold."

They had walked two blocks through the dusk. Although it was still light, the moon, nearly full, shone in the reddening sky. The sidewalk was crowded with children from the buildings on his street, voices rising like bubbles of sound into the trees. His own children would be playing now, too, on their street, and for a moment he had seemed to stumble into a vacant pocket of air, a vacuum where the shouts of his son and his daughter should vibrate. He had never gotten used to being a father, and he had never gotten used to losing his children. Two confusions that together had created this episode of vertigo, Sam Cortez saying somewhere outside the pocket of guilty loss into which Justin had lurched: "Are you all right? Perhaps if you sat on the steps for a moment?"

"I'm fine," Justin had said. He smiled at the stocky young man; pleasant looking, but not his niece's type, he was thinking even as he was recovering. Not hard-edged enough, it didn't seem, to engage the angry emotions of Diana Fry. "Getting over the flu. Still a little woozy, I guess."

Sam Cortez had nodded, lowered his eyes. He knows a lie, Justin thought, and he knows when to leave it alone. A survivor's primary talent. The way you treat a snake or a bear or a person. Life is nothing if not tricky. He could never get Grace to accept that. That most people lied all the time. She would look at him as if she were taking a scan of his brain with her eyes: *Tell me the truth.* Which truth, sweetheart? No wonder she felt more comfortable with death. Death was one truth she could count on.

"So," Justin had said to Sam. They had a table in the back of the bar, a basket of *nachos* between them, mugs of beer. "How can I help you?"

And Sam spoke for a long time, formally, as if delivering a prepared speech, rehearsed for a solemn occasion, as if he were giving a eulogy for his still-living father.

"I grew up in Asunción," he had begun. "My father was—is—a journalist, the editor of a newspaper. In our house, my mother's mahogany harp rested on the landing between the first and second floors. We lived well. When she played, the music would reverberate off the quarry-tile floors and walls, so every chord was multiplied, a whole orchestra of harps grew from that one instrument.

"My father's articles were like that harp. He wrote about the Guana Indians and the Toba-Meskoy tribe. He wrote about the Makas and the Nivakles. 'Under the present government,' he would write, 'we are committing genocide against Paraguay's truest citizens.' He wrote about Mengele, the 'Angel of Death' living in the German quarter of the city. 'Under the present government, Paraguay has become Satan's refuge, a nation where the principle of evil is honored and protected.' I can tell you his words were as true as the notes my mother strummed, and they resounded throughout the country. Students passed his articles among themselves like contraband. Priests who spoke the Indian dialects translated my father's testimony to the landless natives. The police posted his columns like 'Wanted' posters in their stations. When they came to arrest my father in the middle of the night, March 17, 1977, they took my mother's harp and smashed it against the wall, over and over again, until it was nothing but a twisted mass of wood and wire at our feet.

"We were prepared for that night. We knew it would come. From the time I was a small boy, my father and mother had rehearsed with me what my father referred to as his 'kidnapping,' so named because for him the authorities had no authority, the law was lawless. If he were seized—the shock was not that he was, you see, but that for so many years he had been spared— my mother was to contact a 'friendly source' in the American Embassy who would see to it that she and I were transported safely to the United States. On my twelfth birthday—it would be four more years before my father would be imprisoned and my mother and I would begin this vigil thousands of miles away—my father took me into his study. It was a wood-paneled room, the windows heavily draped, good insulation. In Paraguay, the heat is ferocious and the cold numbs. In that room, I always felt under the ground, sealed off from the weather, the wars, actually from the world itself. Books covered one entire wall. Ten feet of books from floor to ceiling and twenty feet across. My father's library was filled with classics, rare editions, reams of words that had survived as if in a time capsule or crypt. His desk was the same mahogany as my mother's harp, and a green leather chair the color of moss matched the sofa that rested beneath the windows. A beautiful room. Beautiful. We sat together on that sofa and my father tamped down the tobacco in his pipe. He was slight even then, small-featured and pale. He looked like a retiring scholar. He spoke quietly. 'Has it been a terrible childhood?' he asked. I said, 'No, it has not been terrible,' though often during those twelve years I had privately cursed him for bringing my mother and me into the center of the nightmare I call 'my country,' for not allowing us to remain in what he named once 'the passive suburbs of wealth and delusion.'

"He said to me, 'I am not an adventurer, you know. Adventurers should not have families, because they cannot give the consistency of affection and imagination that successful family life requires. They are usually preoccupied, or absent. I am very, very interested in you, do you know that? I find you very rewarding.' He was not looking at me when he spoke. But I was not offended. In certain situations, my father was a shy man. I remember thinking: *He is telling me everything that a son needs to know from his father.* If he sounded a bit remote, it was in the manner of a last will and testament, the neutral tone a protection from the grief the words contained. That was the afternoon I fully understood that my father's life was truly endangered by what he wrote. It had not penetrated until that afternoon. 'What do you think you will be when you are a grown man?' he asked. As if I were a distant relative passing through the city whom he might not see again for many years, if ever. I answered immediately. 'A journalist. I'll be a journalist like you.'

"By the end of this year I should be promoted to the Metro section. I have in mind a series of articles about refugee families like my mother and me whose missing member languishes in prison in one of the so-called republics of South America. People here, they do not want to talk about my father. He has been in jail for five years. He has been beaten and shocked and lowered into vats of water up to the point of drowning. His hair has turned completely white, though he is not yet fifty. He has lost a third of his body weight. Three years ago his eyeglasses broke and they do not allow him to have new ones. He cannot read without his glasses. But he sends this message: 'I am writing a book in my head about these years. I have done twenty-thousand words already. Revised twice, permanently recorded. As all my senses diminish my memory intensifies. I remember everything. I remember every single thing.' "

And then Sam Cortez had said to Justin, "He is a superior man." And Justin remembered now the twist of envy he had felt for Sam's good fortune to have a father to whom he could be so devoted. Then a fever of shame for such a niggardly response.

"I can help you," Justin had said. "I can put you in touch with certain people willing to take major risks. You could talk with them. I'll be involved to the degree they think I'd be useful."

Now Justin put his thermal underwear into his suitcase. *Take warm clothes.* A ski jacket, gloves, woolen socks. How far south? Far. He took an inventory, checked bureau and closet again. Suddenly he was exhausted. Without undressing, he stretched out on the bed and slept, the light in his room burning all night, as if for a child frightened of the dark.

On the plane to Miami, Justin remembered his mother's call, his niece's impending wedding, the brother to whom he hadn't spoken in years; a scene from their father's funeral flashed across Justin's brain. All their faces startled him with the suddenness of surprise attack. He wanted to crouch down on the floor of his first-class seat as his family closed in like agents on his well-covered trail. The way he felt—this impulse to hide, these palpitations, this pain in his limbs—it was as if this chase were truly happening outside of his own skin, as if Rose and Karl and Wendell had burst upon him from the cockpit and he was determined to prevent capture at all costs.

Grace had told him repeatedly, "You're blocking. You've got to let yourself grieve. You get as far as the anger, but under the anger is loss, Justin, loss."

"Sweetheart," he'd answered, the endearment souring on his tongue, "any more of that fancy primal pain you recommend so highly and I might just check out entirely."

Now, in the Whisperjet, he tried another one of Grace's therapies, which in her presence he also scorned. From toes to scalp, he willed his body calm, imagined himself in Rock Creek Park, the leaves a dazzling canopy under which he sprawled, the air cool on his face. As good as smoking a joint, he thought. The heart retired.

Relaxed now, he smiled at his anxiety attack. That his family should have been the source of his panic amused him. Wasn't it, in fact, a splendid irony that they were all gathered in this city towards which he flew, yet his presence would not be known to them? They would probably be discussing his absence, the way he had cut his ties to them all, when actually he would be no more than ten minutes from them, talking with a man named Ramon Artigas at the United Airlines baggage-claim counter, beginning a journey that might produce for Diana and Sam a wedding present grander than any of them could ever imagine. That the members of his family should arouse in him more disquiet than the dangers of his political work struck him now as comic, even touching; though sometimes the way in which his family insisted themselves into his consciousness enraged and perplexed him. As if memory were an organism that lived outside him, a separate creature with its own cell structure, metabolism, its own schedule of waking and sleep.

The man in the seat beside him dozed, snoring lightly like an amiable uncle. Justin would have liked to nudge the stranger, share with him this rare and inexplicable affection he felt for the intruder he housed within himself, for the past he carried like a parasite but which now seemed a congenial and domesticated pet. Instead, he joined his fellow passenger in that sort of half-sleep traveling induced, dreams rising up like the clouds the plane entered, lost to itself for a while in the mist, then out again into the visible world.

He dreamed: the Frys' apartment, Wendell and Rose and Karl positioned about the living room like extra pieces of furniture, each person immobile as the tufted tub chairs or the worn damask love seat or the brocade sofa whose frayed arms Rose kept covered with crocheted doilies that Justin loved to throw on the floor. In his dream they sailed like giant snowflakes to the rug; although it was summer, drifts built up along the baseboard, the radiator beneath the window disappeared under a mound of fabric snow. Soon the furniture, too, lay enshrouded and only the people escaped the deluge he had released. He was small, age two or three, his feet bare. To his family, he lifted his arms for rescue, but they gazed on him sternly; a hum of rebuke fell from their mouths. Their hands were folded across their chests. He climbed Karl's legs as if they formed the trunk of a tree, but he found no limb on which to rest; Karl was all pliant surface, a spongy hillock, offering neither resistance nor shelter. Ten feet away, Rose seemed to call to him—"Come here, Justin!"—and he bounded from Karl to his mother, the snow biting at his ankles. But Rose, too, failed his need; she was a tangle of bramble and thorn to him, his name on her lips an ensnaring ruse. He was scratched, bloody; for a moment, the snow felt healing on his mother-wounded skin. Then the cold became its own punishment and he had one more possible haven in this nearly-buried room. Wendell leaned like a ladder against the wall, and Justin lunged for a rung which crumbled in his hands; his foot split the lowest slat. Wherever he reached for his father, the man splintered. From her place at the mantel, Rose cried, "You're destroying him, Justin! You'll be his ruination!" And there was nothing to do but submit to the snow, to this white grave that was his childhood home.

He dreamed: in the room he shared with Karl, an assemblage of traps. Buckets of water poised above the door. The mattresses set with springs which, when triggered, squashed the sleeper inside the bed, which folded back on itself like a sandwich. Each window was wired, to shock. In the closet, the floor gave way under the slightest pressure. Which one of the brothers had rigged the room with such devices? Or was some third party responsible, Karl and Justin pitted against each other, the fraternal alliance violated, ruptured? He could not figure it out. The room rocked like a boat.

He dreamed: yet again, Wendell's funeral. Outside, rain fell, a mist of iron filings or the fingerprinting dust Wendell always carried under his nails. Toomer Brothers': white pillared manse, red bricks showing no trace of Washington pollution, as if this building were impervious to the elements, in an element of its own. In the dream, the funeral parlor turned inside out, like a glove. Justin sat in a pew beneath the sky's perpetual drizzle. He noticed that Rose's hair, to his right, remained dry, as if she, too—like the building's facade—were resistant to weather, airborne poisons, decay. They had never inhabited the same atmosphere, Justin and his mother. In the dream, he remembered nursing at her breast, how it seemed to his infant sensors that a shield resided between him and Rose's body, so that even as he suckled, grabbed at her hair and skin, dug his baby feet into the flesh of her forearm, still she was inaccessible to him, beyond the range of his need. In the dream, he thought: *Am I remembering my infancy, or inventing it for the purposes of this dream?* Grace claimed one could recall even the uterine phase, that no experience vanished. He sat between his mother and his brother; at the front of the chapel, Wendell was "laid out," as Rose called it. Wendell said, "Justin Fry, you have sullied this family's name!" Even in death, he remonstrated? "Traitor!" His voice was huge, quadraphonic, each word reverberated like cannon fire. "Communist!"

Then Justin was awake, all semblance of dream vanished like the last sight of land. His father's funeral rose up undisguised, like a corpse surfacing, the day as it had been: Justin lunging for the coffin, beating on the burnished wood with his fists. "You fucker!" he screamed. "You were after my ass all my life! You're dead, you hear me? You're dead and I'm fucking glad! I've been wishing for it since I was five years old: When's the fucker going to die? You never said a goddamn nice thing to me my whole life, you know that? You never gave a shit about—" Shrieking like a siren, Rose tore at his jacket. "You stop this, Justin! Oh my Lord! Help me, Karl, help your mother!" And Karl had somehow wedged himself between Justin and Wendell's casket, so that all Justin could see now was his brother's face, less scornful than deeply sad, as if it were Justin rather than Wendell whom he had come to mourn. They were pressed in upon each other—Wendell in his casket, Karl, Justin, Rose spread-eagled on his back—and it seemed to Justin, now on the plane as it had that day at the funeral, that they had become a single organism, part living, part dead—a hydra, a monster that called itself "family."

Ramon Artigas was a short, thin man who looked like a jockey to Justin.

"*Señor* Fry," he said.

Behind Artigas, suitcases tumbled from a chute onto a conveyor belt. "My bag," Justin said, and reached into the mass of luggage for his own brown leather case.

All around him, people primed for vacation, cameras around their necks, tennis racquets in canvas cases slung like rifles over their shoulders, children carrying plastic bucket-and-shovel sets in mesh sacks. He thought of Zach and Lisa, made a mental promise to them: a weekend at the the beach when he got back.

Take warm clothes. He knew this journey wasn't over yet. This time his involvement was going to be more complicated, more direct, than it had been on other projects. Other projects: cajoling a friend from Movement days who now worked for the State Department to pass him Xeroxes of classified documents related to the government of Argentina; preparing counterfeit birth certificates and Social Security cards for a tortured-and-released Guatemalan doctor and his family passing through Mexico to Texas; traveling to Chile disguised as a British journalist (Justin is good at accents) in order to ferret out information about the treatment of imprisoned post-Allende leftists. Work of this sort. What he described to his friends in Amnesty and Oxfam and the Human Rights Network Project as "backstaging." He told them, "Think of me as crew. Stagehand, lighting, props. I'm good support staff." They answered, "You should be running this program. With your background, you should be a primary player." But he deferred. If it was not money, neither was it limelight, not anymore, that compelled him to risk himself over and over on behalf of people he seldom knew, but whose suffering felt to him so familiar, whose rage he perceived as concretely as his fingers perceived the suitcase handle they now grasped. All the other reasons. He did not know what they were, exactly, beyond the abstractions of ideology and philosophy. That his niece's fiancé had come to him for help had spurred him on this time, but surely Justin could have done something for Diana—he had always felt close to her, an affinity perhaps genetic, perhaps temperamental—something other than risking his life. What he knew was that he was doing what he was meant to do, wherever that meaning dwelled. Perhaps Grace was right: We reside in mystery, we perish in fact.

Artigas said, "Perhaps we could have a drink in the bar?"

"*Bueno*," Justin said, and the two men stepped onto the escalator and ascended.

In the airport bar, Ramon Artigas emptied the shot glass into his beer, drank down the boilermaker in what appeared to be a single open-gullet swallow. Justin saw Zach making a face after succumbing to a spoonful of Robitussin administered to him by his father. The association relaxed him; Artigas seemed less a stranger now.

"In two hours," he said, "you will take a flight to La Paz. Go to the Hotel El Liberatador. An hour after the plane lands, in the lobby, look for a woman with red hair and a man, small like me, with one arm. They will be sitting on a sofa at the farthest point from the main desk. They are afraid, that is why all this secrecy. They have . . . been through a lot. They will undertake the actual mission in Asunción. Your role requires that you wait for them to return to La Paz. It may be days or weeks; they will know that by the time you arrive. You will set yourself up in the hotel as an agronomy re-searcher, an academic. Now"—and he handed Justin a thick manila envelope—"in here find papers you have written, 'scholarly monographs.' Your subject is 'Latin American Agricultural Models, 1850–1855.' You teach at George Washington University; you are on sabbatical; and so forth."

"And so forth."

It is cold in La Paz, Justin thought. The altitude. He should buy a jar of Vaseline for the nosebleeds.

After Artigas left, Justin remained in the bar, ordered a Coke and a crab cake sandwich. From his wallet, he took out pictures of Grace, Zach, Lisa, as if he were readying for a game of solitaire. He set them in a row on the table before him. With his forefinger, he stroked their features, and his skin remembered the feel of their faces, the slight cleft in Grace's chin, Zach's high brow that gave him a look of perpetual amazement, Lisa's freckle-bridged nose and her tiny pillows of cheeks. Al-though the planes sounded like a sonic bestiary, a jun-gle of jet-fueled roar and whine, Justin heard nothing but the voices of his children and the woman who had once been his wife. He gathered up the pictures, threw a five on the table to cover the bill, headed for the bank of phone booths in the lobby. By the time he got there, he had subdued the need to call them; still, the quarter rested in his palm and before he could pocket it again, he'd dropped it in the slot, dialed information, heard himself asking the operator for his brother's number. "Karl Fry," he said. "Or Fry's Lodge, either one."

With a pen he fished from his pocket, he wrote down on an envelope containing his "scholarship credentials" the digits she intoned. He hung up, waited for the quarter to plink in the change-return slot, used the coin again. After three rings, Karl answered, but Justin said nothing. For a few seconds, a bridge of silence connected them and then that, too, broke: Justin returned his receiver to its cradle. Still, as he walked through the terminal to the ticket counter, Karl's voice—"Hello, hello, is anybody there?"—seemed to speak to Justin through the loudspeakers, stronger than the voices announcing arrivals and departures.

Hello, hello, is anybody there?

In the highest airport in the world, Justin drank a Bolivian beer, Gruzeña, and ate an *empanada*. The spicy meat-filled tart warmed him; he knew it was cold outside and he needed to feel fortified, hardy enough for his imminent encounter with this extreme country. Bolivia: the greatest concentration of cosmic rays on earth. He had read that once when he was just beginning his Latin American studies. The fact had shimmered on the page, as if the words themselves were activated matter. He imagined himself stepping out of the terminal, raising his hand for a cab, and turning into a pile of charged dust before the cabbie even got his engine running.

The cabbie got his engine running.

Still intact, Justin entered the purring car, directed the driver to the hotel where he was to meet the nameless man and woman.

"What's your name?" Justin asked the citified Indian who chauffeured him through the city streets.

The dark-skinned man regarded Justin in the rearview mirror. Justin saw the cool intelligence in the man's eyes. With a practiced finger, the driver smoothed his mustache. Although his face was mostly bearded, Justin observed half-moons of cheek, each cratered with pock marks from some long-ago adolescence.

"I don't have a name, *Señor*," the cabbie said. He grinned. Brown teeth, from cigarettes, no doubt. "Also, I can fly!"

Now he was laughing out loud, his shoulders bouncing like sausages in a pot.

Justin said, "Is it always this foggy in La Paz?"

Through the window, the sky and air and earth were a seamless gray net.

"No, no," the cabbie assured him. "This particular bad day, particular bad." He pulled up in front of El Liberatador. "You like dancing?" the cabbie said. "Up there is the Sky Room." He pointed to the spot in the mist where the building's roof might be. "Up in the clouds, you like to dance?"

"*Sí*," said Justin. "I would like to dance in the clouds. Indeed I would."

[99]

He was too early. At the far end of the lobby, he checked for the couple that matched Artigas' description, but they were not here yet. Well, it gave him time to check in, lie down. He didn't need to risk one of those famous La Paz headaches. At the desk, he signed "Jonathon Friar" in the register, paid for his room with a Traveler's Check. The clerk regarded him—it seemed to Justin—sadly. Or did the man simply have one of those beaglelike faces that simulate dejection? For Grace, body language had the density of Sanskrit, a complex grammar uttered by the bones, the muscles, the nerves. He was not so sure. He was not so certain people amounted to that much, though he was equally unsure that they did not.

He tipped the bellhop. Nothing in the room suggested its particular location in the world. No artifact differentiated it from similar rooms in St. Louis, New York, Paris, Athens. Hotels and graves, he thought. The great equalizers. On the sateen sod, he rested for twenty minutes. Still another hour, but the room was too confining. In the lobby, he sat for a while on one of the modular sofas and watched the tourists. They looked at him as if he were one, too. *So I am*, he mused. *One of life's tourists*. Wasn't that the trouble between him and Grace? He'd always felt like a visitor in her home, wasn't that it? But one not free to leave, he being the husband, he being the father. A perennial resident guest, that had been his sense of those years. Later she would tell him, "You've taken over every inch of this place— your goddamn papers, your files, your photographs plastered on the walls. Where do I fit in here anymore? What's me?" He wanted to explain: *You are you. Your presence, your solace, your smell. All I have here are things. Having misplaced myself.* But he had not been able to articulate it in a way that had made sense to her. Or that she had been prepared to hear.

Now he caught sight of himself in one of the gold-flecked mirror panels. Years had passed; he seemed to grasp this for the first time. Justin Fry was thirty-seven years old. His black hair was laced with gray. His skin was pleated now at eyes and mouth. His eyes—he saw this, for the first time—hooded, the lids having drooped some, an extra fold materialized in each crescent of flesh. He held his hands in front of him: rootlike veins snaked under the surface, his skin was nearly as transparent as water. "Daddy," Zach had asked him, "is it true we're mostly water?" Justin had nodded. "Mostly we are," he'd said, and Zach's face had frozen, until suddenly he'd yelled, "Then how come we don't turn into puddles when we die?" and smacked the rug triumphantly.

Dust, water, earth, stone: What did it matter, that final incarnation? To anyone but a child, what could it possibly matter?

Time for air, Justin thought, though he was not sure what, exactly, was responsible for this constriction in his chest, this strange pressure in his head.

Outside the fog had lifted, like a skirt, a few inches from the ground. A ridge of light rode on the surface of La Paz and Justin stepped into it; his shoes glowed, though the rest of his body hid in haze. He followed his own feet past the banks and restaurants, almost apparitions in the mist. He walked several blocks to the Prado, a spacious avenue on either side of a grassy promenade. He was looking for the contraband market in the heart of La Paz, the bazaar where the vendors had created the "Union of Commercial Smugglers." True capitalism, he had thought the first time he had read about the union. Crime on the up-and-up. What would Wendell have thought of this? Wouldn't it have thrown one more monkey wrench into his notion of justice? He had been a regular tyrant, obsessed, when it came to justice, that father of his.

The smugglers, Justin discovered, were all women. In the land of maschismo, female pirates. Another joke on Wendell. That's what Justin loved about Latin America: Everything was turned upside-down here; Yankee logic fell flat on its presumptuous face. He wandered through the maze of stalls—Spanish, Indian dialects, snatches of gutteral German (the "Butcher of Lyons" was a wealthy businessman here). Languages wove themselves into an invisible net stretched like a roof above his head. Through the skeins, sun poured. The fog had burned away. He saw an old woman sitting in a funnel of sunlight. As he approached her, her burnished skin seemed to deepen, copper to umber, before his eyes. Wrinkles multiplied as he neared her stall. She was ninety, at least. In Spanish, she urged on him the hand-tooled leather belts, the enameled bracelets, the hammered silver boxes lined with silk or velvet. He bought a bracelet for Grace.

"Ah," the old woman announced, as if she were a seer. "Your wife will be very happy."

For Diana and Sam he bought silver candlesticks. For the children, *piñadas* and wooden toys: a train for Zach, for Lisa a dog whose hinged tail wagged when a pellet was placed in its mouth. He would send everything to Grace, ask her to hold the package for him until he returned. He was ready to leave the crowded marketplace—it was time now for the meeting at the hotel, his true purpose for being here, after all, though it seemed no more urgent than anything else to him in this oxygen-deprived state—when he saw a rack of lace shawls, black ones and white, standing before him like an exotic shrub. He plucked a white one from the batch.

When he had been a boy, Rose had had a shawl like this and if she'd leave it coiled on the sofa, he'd snuggle up beside it and stroke the fringe, then drift into a peaceful half-sleep. To this day, he could not resist fringe, the feel of the silky strands between his fingers.

Okay, Rose, he thought, *so I buy you a present. Don't make too much of it. You wouldn't even want it if you knew where I got it. Not Woodward and Lothrop's, you can bet on that.*

"I am not a betting man," Julio said.

They were sitting together in the hotel lobby on the designated settee.

"If I did not believe this project were completely feasible," he went on, "I would not involve myself and my wife."

His wife did not lift her eyes from the hands which stroked a rosary looped in her lap. Justin felt the woman breathing beside him, her shoulder rising and falling against his. They were sitting three abreast, as if on a train, and her breath came fast as a train engine's pant.

"Professor Friar," the man called Julio said in the monotone of rehearsed speech, "while you are conducting your research in La Paz, we will collect the data you need about the Paraguayan economy during the period in which you are interested. Although you are fluent in Spanish, one achieves quicker results in Paraguay if one speaks Guaraní, which of course we do. And we have found the . . . library . . . in Asunción easy to use, providing one talks to the proper clerks. This is paramount. Some are more cooperative than others, of course. We will be making contacts for you with the proper clerks."

"Library clerks."

Sombrero had said, "Perhaps they will change the name to Asunción Library." "Sí," said Julio. "The right clerks will open all the right doors. You shall see. As your . . . researchers . . . we will have access to the most significant material."

"I'm grateful—"

"We are grateful to you. That you should take such an interest in our . . . history. That you should travel so far from your home, from your family."

"I understand that you and your wife—" she stiffened beside him, as if impaled by his voice to the love seat's back—"I understand that you also have been . . . away . . . for an extended period."

"*Sí,*" Julio murmured. He rubbed the stub of arm in his left sleeve. "Away."

The woman's hands locked around the cross. "We had a son who died in the . . . library there." Tears shone like shards in her eyes. "He died there."

They ate dinner in the hotel dining room. The woman cut her husband's veal for him, buttered his bread.

"Luckily," he said, "the right one healed, or she'd have to feed me like a baby."

In his room, Justin double-bolted the door and affixed to the window portable locks he carried with him on his travels. He shut the fiberglass curtains. For twenty minutes, he checked the room for hidden cameras, recorders, listening devices. Clean, so far as he could tell. Such equipment evidenced an ever-developing technology, a growth industry. Julio's wife sat in a chintz-covered Morris chair beside the bed. Julio stood by the window, peering through the crack where the curtains did not quite meet, watching the street below. On the bed, Justin spread the contents of the packet Julio had given him: photographs of Samuel Cortez; a map detailing the route from this hotel to a small airfield in the countryside where a private plane would fly Justin and the freed man to Miami; the keys to a VW van in which Justin would drive Cortez to his wife's apartment in the city, where right now she most likely lay dreaming of such an unlikely reunion.

He absorbed it all, reading it over several times.

"So," said Julio. "You understand."

"I do," Justin said. "Indeed I do."

He was pacing now, back and forth in front of Julio's wife. Her dress stirred in the currents of Justin's stride. Suddenly he stopped, faced the frail, one-armed man.

"Are you sure this is feasible?"

"This is two years of our lives, sir. We have worked patiently here. Getting all the . . . clerks . . . in place. Preparing the . . . methodology. Your participation, for example, was debated among us for many weeks. Researched and evaluated. Is he serious enough? Is his work well-regarded? Does he have the dedication for such an endeavor? I have told you, Professor Friar, I am not a betting man."

Justin picked up a photograph as if it were a card from the pile in a rummy game. He played rummy with Zach all the time. He studied the picture. He remembered his project a number of years ago in Chile. Less dangerous than this one; preparatory, he now saw, to this kind of undertaking. Still, interviewing the relatives of imprisoned leftists at a time when such contacts were being monitored, as if the air itself were rife with invisible spies, had seemed to him foolhardy. He'd confided his doubts to the priest who housed him.

"What is craziness to an American," the priest had instructed, "is courage to a Latino. A necessary courage. Do not forget we are desperate here. We are in a state of perpetual war. If you do not share that sense of emergency, if your soul is not awake to such suffering as we experience, you do not belong among us, whatever your intellectual notions might be. It is your spirit that must be engaged. You must feel yourself one of the sufferers, as Christ teaches. Then you will not doubt the sanity of what we must do here."

"You are still committed, Professor?" It was Julio. "To the project?"

The eyes of Samuel Cortez—prisoner, editor, the father of the man Diana would marry at the end of this week—those eyes regarded Justin. He thought he heard him echo Julio's question.

"Sí," Justin said, answering everyone—Julio, Cortez, the priest, Grace, their children, Diana and Sam, Rose and Wendell and Karl, even himself. He put an arm on Julio's shoulder, smiled through tears at the maimed man. "I am committed."

In the morning he walked with Julio to the Indian produce market on the edge of the Choqueyapu River, and it reminded him of the Potomac, Maine Avenue, the docks he wandered with Lisa and Zach. He'd buy them lunch from a seafood stand, cold shrimp Lisa called "rubber fishes" and Cokes and ice cream bars from the Good Humor truck that parked beside the bait-and-tackle shop.

"Some people believe the river has healing powers," Julio said.

Well, that brought him back. No one could claim that about the Potomac. Not even Wendell, who'd defended just about everything his youngest son chose to criticize. Justin smiled, took his purchase, handed the farmer the requisite number of coins.

"Maybe it just doesn't poison you," he said to Julio. "Maybe that's a miracle in itself."

Julio winked at him. "I'll go for a swim and see if it grows me another arm."

"You see?" Justin said. "Just beginning the research and already thinking like an empiricist."

Indeed, "Professor Friar's" hotel room looked like a researcher's workplace. Julio and his wife had provided him with an almost-antique manual typewriter, a box of manila folders, paper and notecards, pens, two cardboard filing drawers. A dozen well-read books on Latin American agriculture and economic development. Maps for the wall. A ream of graph paper. A convincing ruse, Justin thought. Even an appealing one. What if he had, in fact, become an academic, his professional back properly turned on the world's turmoil, a professor secure in some tenured academic post, wife and children ensconced in a pleasant suburb circa 1950, his mind fixed for years on the Bolivian sugar crop, the nature of its cultivation and yield, 1850–1854?

Last night he could not sleep. He'd pulled a chair to the window and looked out at the darkness. When he was a child, he'd believed the earth changed form at night, that what he could not see by day had disappeared, that the shadows which lengthened across the road were openings to underground caves only accessible in the darkest hours. He hungered to enter those caves. Rose could not shake him from his certainty of a transformed and dangerous world, could not counter his excitement to know it, and she threatened to put a lock on the door to the bedroom he shared with Karl, so fearful was she that Justin would sneak out of the apartment one night and lose himself forever in the city. She never bought the lock, but he knew she lay in bed for years half asleep, half awake, so attuned to his movements that a bedspring's squeak could bring her in an instant to his doorway: "Justin? Are you all right?" she'd whisper, and if he didn't answer, she'd come to his side and poke him awake, all to assure herself of his well-being. Remembering those visitations, he'd felt surprisingly tender toward her, toward her vigilance on his behalf.

Last night he watched an errant paper bag rise and fall on a gust of cold wind. How did the bag escape the street sweepers, he had wondered, whom he'd observed shouldering their brooms like rifles, lowering them to their work with the discipline of soldiers?

Not a bad symbol for his own life, he'd mused, that wind-tossed debris. How strongly he'd believed he could mount History and ride it out of his family's homestead, but there was no road and History had no body for him to grasp—only this swirl of events, violent squalls and momentary calmings, persecutors and victims alike caught in the invisible currents, people not land dwellers at all, but creatures of the ungovernable white-water air. Even street sweepers could be lifted up at any moment, wrenched from their solid work. Alone in the night in a strange country, he had seen them all—his parents, his brother, Diana, Florence, Charlotte, whom he did not know, Grace and their children, himself—he'd seen them wheeling through the emptiness, and he had been afraid for them all, even

Wendell; and he had cried for them all for the first time, for the Frys, for the family of which he was, even this far away, one.

Now Julio said, "The librarian in the economics room tells me he plans to work tonight, very late into the night, on his catalogs, and he has most graciously invited us . . . your assistants . . . to use the facilities of the library while he is there, assuming we can get to Asunción ahead of schedule. I told him of course. So we will get a head start, you see, on our project; we will not need to wait until Monday, as we had anticipated. We will have excellent access. I have told him to expect us sometime after dark, my wife and me."

Outside the city, the streetlamps disappear.

Behind the wheel of a rented car, Justin Fry keeps his eyes fixed on the sky's flares—moon and stars a map he follows as if he were already airborne, as if he had left the earth behind him and risen above the clouds.

La Paz recedes and disappears.

Although he is trembling—a car at his rear travels so closely for almost a mile that Justin is sure he is being followed and he knows that being followed in South America does not result in a ticket for speeding—still the three-mile journey to the field where the plane waits is actually as uneventful as the Sunday rides he had to take as a boy: Wendell fixed on the road with the singular intensity of a man navigating over the perilous route from whose dangers he was always, somehow, spared. He is more like his father than he knows, or will admit to.

Though now his terror is sensible, the fantasies of disaster reasonable for a man on this particular trip: He imagines mines exploding under his wheels, sudden roadblocks, machine-gun fire raining down on him from all sides. In fact, he arrives safely at the field and sees there the truck he has been instructed to expect—a farmer's pickup truck, usually engaged in the transport of sugar cane from the altiplano to the city, this time with another cargo, human, clambering over the truck's slatted sides to the ground. And Julio's voice coming from the cab as Justin follows the former prisoner, Samuel Cortez, up the steps of the plane: *"Gracias, amigo. Gracias, hermano."*

Friend, brother. Justin takes the words aboard. Inside, it is as dark as it is on the field, only a few flares on the makeshift runway visible through the steamed-over windows. Julio's truck dissolves to vapor, the car Justin drove from La Paz vanishes. The plane gathers speed on the ground. They leave the earth. Samuel Cortez prays aloud in a hushed jabber that gathers in volume as the plane ascends, until finally he is shouting in such joyous and sustained resonance that it seems to Justin the speech of survivors is fuel enough to keep an airplane aloft, to propel it from danger to safety, into that region the newly freed properly name "the rest of my life."

DIANA

GUYS KILL ME.

You make it with someone a couple of times and he thinks he's got a lifetime lease on your body.

I'm marrying Sam, but Wayne Cutler won't leave me alone.

My mother says, "You bring it on yourself, Diana."

"Oh, really?" I say. "How exactly do I do that?"

"Males are easily aroused, Diana. This is a known fact."

In my mother's way of thinking, men are a collection of dangers you spend your time trying to avoid.

You should see her at the bus stop in the morning, on her way to her job at the hospital: a white uniformed sentry, feet together, eyes pinned on the road, her purse clutched like a gun in front of her chest. Everything about my mother says: *Don't come one step closer or I'll shoot.*

And she's a nurse.

Florence L. Fry, R.N. Doesn't that slay you?

What I tell her is, "I'm not responsible for Wayne's hormones, *he* is."

I'm careful not to say "cock," but even so she lays a hand to her forehead to let me know a sudden pain is pressing on the nerves behind her eyes. She turns on migraines like some people yawn in your face.

What I have to admit, though, is I do come on to guys. I like to. I like to see them blush and lean their bodies into you the least bit. Something no one notices who isn't watching, but you know it means that every cell of theirs is singing your name. I like that.

Liked.

Wayne Cutler says I'm a whore and he loves me.

Sam says, "Loneliness drove you so far away from yourself, it did not matter who you were with. In fact, you were not with anyone."

Sam is the one I'm going to marry. Samuel J. Cortez is how his by-line reads in the paper. He grew up in South America—Paraguay—but he came here with his mother four years ago and his English is almost normal. He's had stories in the Miami *Herald* with his name printed. He went to college, which is more than you can say for Wayne. Wayne's a bartender at The Cat's Meow.

He pumps iron and smokes dope. He's a zero in everything but sex. And I don't think you should marry someone just because he turns you on.

Not that Sam doesn't. I mean, it's fine. It's good enough. Sometimes I think I'd be happy if I never fucked anyone again in my life.

What I like best about being with Sam is afterwards, the way he curves his body into a boat and I curl into it, safe as a baby. What's safe about being turned on? Nothing.

I would never tell my mother this.

She'd gloat. "Oh," she'd say, "so Miss Fun-and-Games is getting careful after all? Too bad you didn't listen to me years ago when you still had a reputation worth protecting."

I don't think I've been bad. Just foolish. Not looking out for my own interests. Twelve years of Catholic schools, but the idea of sin never made an impression on me.

Sam says, "Religion is a false system based on real assumptions."

"You sound like my uncle," I told him the first time he started talking philosophy like that.

"Your uncle?"

"Justin Fry," I said.

I got the usual reaction: wide eyes, dropped jaw. "*The* Justin Fry?"

"*The* Justin Fry," I said.

I was a little girl when he was famous. He was on the tube all the time. This was the sixties. I have a scrapbook filled with clippings about him. All the rallies he organized—Berkeley, Ann Arbor, Harvard, places you might just have happened to hear of. The papers printed his speeches. I have pictures of him getting arrested at the White House and the Pentagon, and then his trial. What they got him for was perjury. He'd been in court a few years earlier and said he hadn't forged documents for friends in the Movement who were in hiding, but he had: phony birth certificates, diplomas, driver's licenses, passports. After his trial, they disbarred him and sent him to detox instead of jail.

Once I was visiting my grandmother in D.C. and Justin came to see me. I asked him what detox was like. I already knew some kids who were hooked.

"Jail would have been much more pleasant," he said.

I knew he wasn't trying to give me a scare trip. I could tell from his face and his voice that he meant what he said.

"I wish you'd come to Florida sometime," I said. "I really miss you."

He and my father are brothers, right? Cain and Abel. And I know who sold out who. Justin gets a bad rap in my family. My father likes to say, "Your uncle and I just don't see eye to eye on things." That's not the reason they don't talk. I know the reason. I know what my father did. Someday he'll get me mad enough and I'll tell him I know. Mr. Sweet and Gentle. Mr. Fair. Just like he was fair to my mother and me. Mr. Hypocrite.

Six months after I saw him in Washington, Justin called me at work from the Miami airport. I met him there for lunch. He was going to Brazil, he said.

"Do you know anything about Latin America," he wanted to know. "About the political situation?"

I said I didn't know about the political situation in Miami, Florida.

He didn't consider that a cute remark.

"Open your eyes," he said. "Learn how the world operates, Diana."

He made me think. He gave me a pile of paperbacks all marked up with his own notes in the margins. Karl Marx, Herbert Marcuse, Richard Sennett. The diary of a poor woman in Brazil called *Child of the Darkness*. I read them all, and they weren't exactly pleasure reading. I read the diary twice.

Justin said, "We'll talk about them when you're finished. I'll be back through Miami in three weeks."

He never called. That was over two years ago. *He never called me.*

"I would like to meet your uncle someday," Sam said. "He has a fine mind, a very fine political intelligence."

Sam gives me books to read, too. He wants me to go back to college. I tell him I will after we're married, but I probably won't.

I wait tables at Miller's—dinner shift, five to midnight. The pay stinks, but I make good tips. You learn how to work it. Sam is always after me to quit, but I tell him it's good as anything until I decide what I want to take up in school. The truth is, I'm just used to it.

Wayne is used to dope. Grass, mostly. Once in a while, he gets his hands on some coke and then he's really flying.

I used to do dope, but not since Sam.

Sometimes he's so straight, I want to say fuck off, but I don't.

Wayne was waiting for me last week in the parking lot out back when I got off.

"Let me talk to you for ten minutes," he said.

The sodium lamps made him look like a ghost of himself. I wanted to touch him all over to see if he were real or not. The trash bins were open and the air smelled of rotting garbage. You would never know from there that out front the place is thick with hibiscus, azaleas, flowering cacti.

"You still want me," Wayne said. "It's written all over you."

"Like I want poison," I said. "Now just let me—"

I felt wherever Wayne touched me, I would turn into a ghost like him, and even when the sun rose over the ocean three blocks down, and the beach filled with people, both of us would still be lost in a dead world.

Curt came out then. He's night manager, and closes up the register when Mr. Miller's not around. Sometimes Curt passes me a ten or a twenty. Sometimes I let him squeeze my ass in the kitchen. You learn how to work it.

I said, "Hey, Curt," and Wayne let go of me fast.

"You still want me," he said, like that was the beginning of something instead of the end.

Wayne's teeth are perfect. He could do toothpaste commercials. He could do other kinds, too. Wayne looks like those statues of naked men they have in art museums. When I was with Wayne, I touched him all over, same as if he was one of those statues and I was into art. I wasn't. I was into Wayne.

Bad move. He is all fucked up. First time I was with him, he tells me his life story.

"Hey," I said. "How come you're being so personal with a stranger?" I wished he'd turn out the lights again. But he wanted to talk.

"You know what?" he said.

He was shredding cigarette filters in the ashtray balanced on his chest.

"My daddy left us when I was four years old and I didn't see him again until last year," Wayne said. "He came all the way from California in his silver Eldorado, and you know what? He had his trunk fitted up into a wet bar. No shit. Did I want a drink, he asked me. I told him, 'You go back to your sweet little family in L.A. and take your fucking bar-on-wheels with you, you bastard.'"

Wayne got so worked up remembering, he threw the ashtray against the wall. It broke into pieces. Jagged stars all over the rug.

"Hey," I said. "Calm down."

"I could break everything in this room," he said. "I could total it."

He could.

"You were probably lucky to be rid of him," I said. "He probably did you and your mother a favor."

He said, "Oh, is that how you worked out your shit? Pulled a con on yourself like that?"

"Who's talking about me?" I hoisted the sheet up over my breasts.

Wayne yanked it back down. "Everybody's always talking about theirselves. Even when they say they're not. Don't you know that yet?"

When Wayne's around, I don't know what I know.

"I don't con myself about anything," he said. "Not about him and not about her neither. My mother was always in cahoots against me and my father. She hates men. So he left. I was four, five, like that. I don't hold it against him. Just for not taking me. I mean, we was both guys. But he left me with my mother and Jeanine, and I had to take all their crap for me and for him, too. He left me to take it for both of us."

"Wayne, it's not my business," I said. But he didn't hear me.

"For a while, I thought I didn't like girls at all," he said. "No shit. Like, around thirteen and fourteen, guys would always be ripping off skin mags from the drugstore and creaming over the broads. I'd say, 'Look at those tits, man!' But I wasn't interested. I used to wake up in the middle of the night and think I was a fag or something. Like, I was down on women. But I was down on guys, too. I didn't have much use for anyone, is the truth. You want to know something that will shock the pants off you, Diana Fry? I figured to be a monk for a while, the kind that lives in those huts they have, off alone; they don't eat in the main monastery or nothing. Real hermits. I thought, I'll get me a dog and go be one of them monks and everyone can go fuck theirselves."

[122]

I kissed his chest. "I guess you're not a monk," I said.

"Nah. I fucked about five or six women before you. I don't know, one day they just started to turn me on. I liked it and I didn't. I liked not being a fag, I can tell you that. If that had come off, I'd have blown my brains out. Fags are lowlife, you know? Like, I'm not exactly Mr. Clean, but I got some principles. Fags, they could be animals if they walked on all fours, that's the only thing different. So I was glad I was doing it with broads. But I didn't like it that much."

He turned on his side and pulled my face to his, His eyes changed colors, the light in them shifting kaleidoscopes.

"I didn't like it until you," he said. "I wouldn't even put you on the top of the list looks-wise. I've had prettier. And you could use a little more meat on your bones."

He was running his other hand down my side, my leg.

He said, "But you talk to me right. Like, we're really having a good talk now, right? I'm telling you about my old man. I never told no one about him. I kept that closed. But I'm telling you, right?"

"You're hurting me, Wayne," I said. He was squeezing my chin, pressing my lip into my teeth. "I need a cigarette." So he lit one for both of us. I moved away from him some, but he didn't notice. He was lost in his story again, that and the cigarette.

"He comes back when I'm eighteen and it's like he's been on a business trip or off in the Army or something. He never sent one letter or check or nothing. My mother spends all those years working her butt off at the airport—she's on maintenance there. Meaning she cleans the johns. I got my differences with her, but he could have sent us some goddamn money. That fucker. He drives up in his monster Caddie, and like I said. I'm sitting on the stoop, having a smoke. He gets out of the goddamn Fleetwood and I see who he is right off. You know your own face when you see it. He says to me "Wayne." He's grinning. He sticks out his hand and I stare at it. He gives me a look that says: *Okay, I got something even better for you.* Like he's a salesman or something. Bounces back to the Caddie. The trunk's all fit up for a bar. He wants us to have this drink right outside the house. "What's your pleasure, son?" he says. Fourteen years and he wants to play Popsie again. I told him what to do with his booze. I told him. The neighbors had to call the cops to shut me up. I was on a tear. I was going crazy. I had him up against the front grille with his arms pinned back on the hood and I was letting out fourteen years of crap on him. His face was the color of the car, his eyes bulged out like a frog's. I'm hollering bloody murder. Ma's inside hiding, Jeanine's on the front stoop crying. I think about it, I get the shakes."

He reached across the sheet for my hand. It was true, he was like jelly. His fingers.

"So you know what happens?" he said. "The cops come. I let up on him and he jumps in that Caddie and guns it like it was a Corvette or something. He takes off like a bat out of hell. My mother comes running out of the house and she's screaming at the cops, 'He's gone crazy!' So they take me in for observation. After three days, she tries to get them to keep me there longer. You hear that? My own mother wants to keep me in a fucking nuthouse! They had people walking around thought they was Jesus and Hitler and Elvis. One guy yanked out the hair from his head and eyebrows; he had just two scars over his eyes. They had some couldn't eat by theirselves or go to the bathroom. You're trying to watch TV in the dayroom, forget where you are for a while, and some guy next to you, he's got his hand right there and you can see the stain. Shit. And she wants me in there for months, years. My own mother. I had to take her crap all my fucking life."

He was shaking so bad, he couldn't even light another cigarette. I reached across him for the matches and he pulled me down on top of him.

"Don't ever give me crap, Diana," he said into my ear. "Don't get me mad at you. You're the best. I don't never want to hurt you or nothing."

"Then I guess you won't," I said, and finally he let me turn out the lights again.

The other night Sam was typing at the kitchen table. I came up behind him and kissed him on the neck. He didn't miss a word. I reached down between his legs and gave him a squeeze.

"Remember me?" I said.

He moved my hand away like it was something that had fallen into his lap by accident.

"Diana," he said, not even looking up from his typewriter, "I'm working."

After we're married, what will I do on a night like this when Sam's nothing but words on a page?

"You'll go to college," he says. "Study. Make friends. You'll visit your family."

I'm not dumb, but I can't stand school. I tried college for one semester last year. My sociology teacher was crazy about me. Not like that. He liked my questions is what I mean. He didn't think that I was a smart ass. Most teachers do, which means I have to muzzle myself. That, or fight them when they try to shut me up. But this one let me talk. "Your anger's wonderful," he said. "But you should channel it. You could do some fine research if you trained that mind."

"Research about what?"

"The things that make you angry," he said. "Cultural hypocrisy, class prejudices, sexism—"

"Don't get fancy," I said. "My mother makes me angry. Not having any money makes me angry. Wayne Cutler makes me angry."

"You don't think other people have similar problems? You don't see yourself as a societal—"

"You remind me of my uncle."

"Your uncle."

He thought I was changing the subject on him, but I wasn't.

"Justin Fry."

He lifted his brows. "I should have recognized the—"

"Except he'd never get himself locked up in a rat

hole like this for an office and he'd never turn himself into a word machine and—"

"I haven't heard much about him for some years," he said, like I wasn't in the middle of insulting him. "How is he?"

"I don't know. He . . . we're not in touch. But he had the same ideas as—"

Then I started bawling. Bolted. Summa cum nothing.

So much for college.

Friends and family: more dead ends. I haven't had friends since D.C. I've run around with this group or that, but nothing tight. I just don't like people much anymore. What's the point? You set yourself up. Sam says I just haven't met the right people yet. Right for what? Anyone can let you down. Anyone can disappoint you. Even Sam might.

As for family, my mother's a witch and my father is spacey as hell. My stepmother, Charlotte, is okay, but she's always tied up with Mary. The way Mary smiles at you, like you're both in on the same moron joke. A retarded stepsister. I can't stand to be around her. Justin I really like, but he split. I shouldn't say split, really; he had good reason. My mother told me. She was pissed at my father once and she said, "A man who would turn in his brother, what can you depend on him for?" She watched me. She knew how I'd take it. In my family, everyone rats on everyone else. My grandmother's cool, but she's a thousand miles away and letters don't do it for me. I stopped writing her a few months after we moved down. Once I called her on the phone.

"Come and get me," I said. "I hate it here."

"I'm not able," she said. "That would be kidnapping."

She took deep breaths, like it was a stethoscope instead of a telephone pressed up to her ear.

"Are you all right?" I said. "Are you sick?"

"Sick at heart," she said. "Diana, you promise me you'll be happy with your mother in Florida. You promise me you'll give your new life a chance."

I said I was sorry I had upset her. I was sorry, all right. For myself. When I hung up, I knew she would never rescue me. I'd crossed my father off my list, and Justin, and now I crossed off my grandmother.

End of list.

I was where I'd been all along without knowing it: alone.

"You act like you're the only person in the world," my mother likes to tell me.

"Maybe I am," I said once. "Maybe all the rest of you are paper dolls. Remember how I used to play with paper dolls?" I was cutting my toenails. "Better hold on to your head," I said, and waved the scissors at her like a sword.

"I'll have you locked up!" she screamed, and a minute later I could hear her on the phone to my father.

Sam says I was trying everything to bring them back together. "By turning yourself into a constant problem to them, by sacrificing your dignity even, you ensured their continuing communication. You see? Anything to have them in touch."

"Maybe I'm just not very nice," I said. "Could you live with something that boring?"

"No," he said. "Could you?"

This is how we met:

Sam would come into Miller's for dinner two or three times a week. When he ordered, he talked like I was going out of my way for him and he was grateful.

You can tell a lot about a man from how he talks to waitresses.

But he would watch me. I like to be looked at when it's my idea. Otherwise, it feels like cobwebs catching onto my hair, my blouse, my nylons. You have to wear nylons at Miller's. One night I brought him his fried-shrimp platter and said, "I wish you'd cut it out."

He didn't say, "Cut out what?"

He didn't say, "C'mon, baby, be nice."

He said, "I didn't mean to offend you."

"Well Jesus," I said. "Night after night. At least you could have asked me out or something."

"I was thinking about how to introduce myself."

Like I was the Queen of England. I thought, *Oh, you sucker.* Then I thought, *Well, why not?*

I said, "I'm Diana Fry. What's your name?"

I'll tell you what he did. He stood up. He put his hand out for me to shake it. Manners make me nervous. My parents are nothing but "please" and "thank you" and "if you would be so kind," and underneath she's knifing you to ribbons and he's getting ready to cut out. At least that's how it turned out for me. Let me tell you, I have had it up to here with manners, but the look in Sam's eyes said: *This kindness is dependable.*

"Why me?" I said, like we had agreed to something.

"In my country," he said, "the Gumaní Indians have a saying: 'Live like the fisherman who believes in depths he cannot see.' "

"And catches it from sharks," I said.

He waited until I got off work.

"I'll take you home," he said.

"My mother's there."

"I don't plan to come in."

"What is this?" I said.

"There are other ways to live, Diana."

I did my number on him, out there in the parking lot, moving my body against his the way they like, licking his ear. He kept his hands in his pocket.

"I get it," I said. "You're gay."

"Not at all," he said, and I could tell from the huskiness in his voice that he had a feeling for me. "But I'm not ready to jump into bed with you yet."

Yet. As long as we'd get to it. It's what I knew how to do.

Later, Sam would say, "Why don't you take yourself more seriously?"

"Why should I? Mostly I like to party."

"Your eyes are sad and intelligent."

I tried to laugh that one off. But the laughing turned into crying.

"What is this," I said, "shrink time? I thought your business was newspaper work."

Something Sam said:

"You should know your own history like you know your country's. Memory gives you power over your life. In Paraguay my father is in prison because he won't 'forget' what they want him to. In some places, they kill you for knowing what you know and remembering it."

Nothing I remember is worth killing me for. My life is small. I can sum it up easy: Once I was happy, then I wasn't.

In D.C. I was a happy kid. Nobody believes me. The guys I've been with, they say, "You probably got knocked around when you were little," or "Your old man run around? Or your old lady?" Like they have it all figured out.

I'm not the type to remember much. But sometimes when I'm with Sam, afterwards, I close my eyes and the past comes back in pictures. It's like a flick. I'm in the old house in D.C. Nothing fancy. Three-bedroom Cape Cod, a kitchen hardly bigger than a closet. Nothing special. It's past five, say. Winter. I miss winter. Piles of old snow like dirty laundry along the curb. The sky's dust-gray. I watch the sparrow at the feeder outside our kitchen window. My father's big on feeders. That, and giving things away to Goodwill and the Salvation Army. My mother's a nut for house sales, brings home knickknacks and gadgets by the bagful. Sometimes I go with her on Saturdays. She'll get excited over a potato peeler, over a broken pair of shoe trees. Once we had five sets of Parcheesi because she kept picking them up "for nothing." She fills the place up and my father empties it out. I figured it was their routine. It seemed to me like they had a plan, like they were working together, getting things to the right people at the right time. Wrong. They were doing trips on each other. I didn't figure it out until later. Until too late. They never yelled.

Meanwhile, she has a stew bubbling on the stove. I smell sage. I smell celery. She shakes in Kitchen Bouquet and the smell of it fizzes like a tiny rocket through the air.

Sam told me once, "The strongest memories are smells. Ask people who have been in war what they remember. They'll tell you burning tar, smoke, the smell of corpses. Ask someone who's been in prison. Always the same: urine."

I'm coloring at the kitchen table. The crayons smell like gasoline.

My mother heats up the iron. She's ironing her uniforms while she listens to the call-in show on the radio.

A woman says, "My name is Louise, and in all my Christmas presents this year, I'm including nylon netting because it's just the best thing for washing dishes ever."

My mother says, "And try it for the bathroom tile, Louise, for the grouting."

That's right. She talks to the talkers, like they're right in the kitchen with us. But I like that. It seems friendly. What does a kid know?

Then my father comes home. He works for the government in a big office divided up like an egg carton into little sections, one for each person. He took me there once and I stapled fifty copies of a report he wrote. He smiles at each of us, gets himself a cream soda, and sits down like the little statue of Buddha my mother keeps on her dresser. He looks like one of those monks who never speak. I saw pictures of them in *Life* magazine. But I like that. His silence makes me calm. I don't feel ignored, because of how he smiles. If I go and sit beside him, he won't say anything, but he'll put one arm around me and give my shoulder squeezes while he sips his soda and stares out the window at the magnolia trees in the front yard.

Like I said, I was happy.

I look at my comic book. I rest an elbow on his knee. His breath brushes my hair.

There's my mother, yammering to the radio, and my father in some kind of trance until dinner, and I'm happy.

Nobody's yelling. Nobody's cursing each other out. Seemed nice to me. What does a kid know.

"It was all in the undercurrents," my mother said when I asked her what happened. "It was like walking barefoot on shells."

I never got cut is all I know. Maybe I made myself not notice everything that wasn't right. Maybe.

And we had nice furniture in that house. That was another thing. He gave it all to her when he left and she sold every stick before we moved down here. Every stick. Even my maple dresser with the mirror attached. Even the antique walnut rocker with the creweled seat where I rocked my doll to sleep. Even the hand-tooled leather hassock Justin brought us from Mexico. The whole kit and caboodle. Gone in one day to strangers traipsing through the rooms I'd lived in all my life. I wanted to ax everything to splinters, rather than let her sell it like that.

"Sell me, too," I told her. "Do it right if you're going to do it."

"Talk to me when you're grown," she said. "Until then, mind your own business."

She went on making change, writing out receipts.

"Well, your grandmother called this morning," my mother said. "She's at your father's."

She banged out yesterday's coffee grounds on a piece of newspaper. "Wants you to telephone her."

She was buttering toast like a bricklayer piling on cement. She cracked eggs hard enough to break open stones.

"I think I'll take her to lunch," I said. This was yesterday.

She slammed down a mug in front of me on the table. If it had had coffee in it, I would have been scalded.

"You never invite *me* to lunch," my mother said.

"I live with you," I said. "I see you all the time."

"She was always butting in."

"She was nice to me."

"She put ideas into your head. That I was doing things wrong."

[134]

"She did not."

"I know how she does, Diana. Don't tell me otherwise. Always criticizing. Always looking for a person's weak spot. Like she's perfection herself. And Wendell was even worse. Well, look how their children turned out, look—"

"You look," I said. I'd had it with her and it wasn't even 9:00 A.M. "You look all you want."

I was halfway out the front door when she yelled, "And don't go talking to her about me, you hear?"

I heard and heard and heard. Sometimes that voice comes at me when I'm far away from her. Like she's made a tape of herself and planted it inside my brain. It's louder than anything. Even sex. I mean, I used to be making it with a guy, both of us high as kites, hard rock blasting in our ears, and still she'd be picking on me, same as if she was right in the room.

But not with Sam. That's the big reason I decided to marry him. He shut her up. My head is more my own when I'm with Sam.

"Hey, Grandma!"

I was in a pay phone in a filling station. Eddie, who works there, eyed me from the pumps. I turned my back on him.

"Well, if it isn't the bride-to-be herself!" said Grandma. "When am I going to see your beautiful face?"

"We could have lunch," I said. "I could pick you up at eleven or so."

"Lunch on the town! Sounds perfect to me, dear.

I'd better check with Charlotte and make sure nothing else is planned here. Hold on, now."

I heard chatter: Charlotte, Daddy, Grandma. I heard Mary making sounds of her own. I pressed the receiver closer to their voices. But still I couldn't make out a word.

What were they saying?

What kinds of plans could they have?

What was it like in that house?

I've only been there a few times. They always invite me, but I never go. Whenever I try to imagine it, all I get is buzz and static. No pictures. Like I was never even inside once. Some flat shapes I hardly recognize. Chairs, maybe. Could be people or trees or space in a doorway, for all I know. Who cares? They don't have anything to do with me.

I was glad when my father moved down here. Not that we had much to say to each other. We'd have dinner near the rooming house where he lived, and then we'd sit on the porch there and look at the ocean. Then we'd get on a bus and go back to my mother's. Not exactly excitement. Once I said, "I wish you had a real place, not just a room. So I could have some of my stuff where you live."

So I could come and live with you, is what I meant.

"Oh, I intend that," he said. "Once I learn enough about the hotel business, I plan to look for a better position, Diana. It's just that now . . . well, maintenance work doesn't pay very well, you see. I—"

Then he was off dreaming somewhere. He gets

this look and you know he wouldn't hear you if you screamed in his ear. He's gone.

So what happens? He meets Charlotte and they get married and buy themselves this falling-down house with six cottages on the grounds. You have to walk a year to get to the beach. No wonder the people who owned it before went bust. Fry's Lodge, they call it. They live in the house and rent out the cabins. When they can. At first I was happy about it. Charlotte's nice. But Mary. I'm not interested in a retarded stepsister. I'm not interested in a stepsister at all, but why did he have to get me one who can't even talk in sentences? He couldn't hack it with me and my mother, but living with a moron, that he can handle. She even calls him "Daddy." When I heard that, I said: *Forget it.* Then I find out what he did to Justin. After a while, you get the picture. You learn. You don't always like what you learn.

You know where I made it that first time with Wayne? Cabin #4. Climbed in the window. Right under their noses.

"Lunch it is!" Grandma said. "I'm going to take my bath right now. I'll be ready right on the dot. I don't dawdle like a lot of old ladies."

Before my parents split up, and we still lived in D.C., I used to go to Grandma's on Sunday morning, and she'd visit us once or twice a week. Rose Fry. I'd see her name on her apartment door and ring the buzzer, and you'd think it was Christmas, the way she'd grin. She'd open the door and I'd smell her cologne, Evening in Paris. She let me play dress-up in her room.

"Who's this, Grandma?"

She had a picture on her dresser in a fancy frame.

"That's your Grandpa Wendell when he was a young man. You only knew him when he was old and sick. I wanted us to see him handsome. Wasn't he handsome?"

I said, "He looks like Uncle Justin."

Grandma's chin puckered. Her eyes blurred. "They could never see a single similarity. Wouldn't. They were blind to each other. Yet there they were, two peas in a pod."

She hugged me to her. When she hugged me, she'd make a place in her body for me to fit. Or else it felt like that. Her bones gave, so I could be comfortable. In my mother, nothing bends or moves. Oh, I loved those Sunday morning visits to Grandma's place! My father would sit in the blue wing chair by the window. Light would come through the sheers and turn him golden. He was always pale, except in that chair. I'd sit on the sofa, brown velvet, pillows Grandma needlepointed with flowers, fruit, ladies with parasols. Grandma would come in from the kitchen with a tray of pastries, coffee for her and my father, milk for me. She'd use her good dishes.

"Everytime you come, it's a holiday," she'd say. "I feel festive soon as you walk in the door."

On the day I went to say good-bye to her, she had the china out again. Making us shirred eggs and sausage.

"This isn't a holiday," I said. "This is the day I have to move."

She went on preparing the brunch. "Your mother will be down there for a month, no longer than a nice vacation, and she'll recognize her mistake. Taking you away from your father and me. From your friends. Her feelings are hurt is all. She's not seeing things clear."

My father said, "Mother, I don't think you should mislead Diana."

"Diana can make up her own mind," I said.

But he was right. She gave me false hopes. That first month in Miami, I kept waiting for my mother to change her mind. It didn't happen. I called up Grandma collect.

"I want you to come and get me," I said.

"I can't. That would be kidnapping."

"But I'm asking. You're my grandmother. You wouldn't be stealing me against my will."

"It isn't so simple, Diana," she said.

But it was. She didn't want me enough, and neither did my father. Even when he moved down from D.C., he made sure he lived in a place where there wasn't room for me. My mother didn't really want me either, but what would people say about a woman who gave up her kid? If Florence Fry cares about anything, it's what people think.

I told this all to Sam once and he said, "Self-pity does not become you. Stand in their shoes."

"What if they don't fit?" I said.

"I did not say forgiveness was comfortable. Only that it was necessary."

I said, "You know what, Cortez? You know what

I think? I think you should have your own section in Bartlett's."

Fry's Lodge.

The driveway's covered with pebbles and shells. The shells never stop breaking. Every time you drive over them, they get a little more crushed.

I parked at the edge, by the road, and blew my horn for Grandma.

I knew. I'd get a call later from my father.

"Now why didn't you come inside and visit for a while?" he'd say. "It's a good thing you're getting married day after tomorrow, or no telling when we might see you next."

Ever since he married Charlotte, he says "we." Like he doesn't exist anymore. CharlotteKarlMary.

I watched Grandma walk up the drive. She was a stitch: big hat with streamers down her back, too much rouge; and she walked in those high heels like they were her first pair.

"You look gorgeous," I told her, opening the car door for her to get in. She did a pirouette for me.

"I guess we know where you got your good looks," she said.

She winked at me, and got in the passenger's side. She gave me a hug over the gear shift. Evening in Paris.

Suddenly: "Di, Di, Di!"

It was Mary. Jesus. Jumping up and down like a kangaroo on the front porch. I did not want this today. I pretended not to hear, but Grandma put her hand on my arm when I shifted into reverse. "I believe Mary needs to see me," she said, like we both didn't know I was the one the shrieks were for.

I shrugged. "I'll just wait here," I said. I looked straight ahead. The sun was bleeding out around the edges of the clouds. Gauze-covered wounds. It was almost noon.

"Well, isn't this unusual?" Grandma said.

We were sitting in the restaurant at the Deauville. The beach was empty. The sky was dark now and the ocean was kicking.

Wayne loves storms. He told me once, "You know what my favorite was? Hurricane Inez."

"What's unusual?" I said to Grandma.

"Fruit in my chicken salad. Pieces of orange and pineapple. Very tropical."

I picked at my stuffed avocado.

"But you're not hungry at all," she said. "Of course, you wouldn't be. You're getting married day after tomorrow. You're scared to death."

"Who says."

"Who isn't?" she said. "I didn't sleep a minute the night before my wedding. Forget all that dream-come-true business. It's a gamble and everybody knows that, too. Everybody."

I was ready to open up to her. I was ready to tell her about Sam and his father and Wayne. I was ready to tell her that I was so antsy about this wedding, I wouldn't have minded climbing out of my body, leaving it right on that beach and the rest of me, the invisible part, could take off for wherever I damned pleased. L.A., maybe. Timbuktu. Someday I'd get another body, but not right away. I'd take my time about it.

I was ready to tell her everything when she said, "Now your father and Charlotte seem very happy to me. I had my doubts from afar, but this visit has put them to rest. Right in your own family you have an example of a marriage that's working out well."

If she thought I wanted my life to be anything like Charlotte's—a husband who's a total fuck-up and a retard for a kid—oh Jesus. I would rather be dead or getting high with Wayne, telling the future to shove it, to hell with dreams that never have a chance because of the real stuff life dishes out.

She looked so stupid in that hat.

The Cat's Meow is two blocks from Miller's. I park my Chevette in the restaurant lot and walk to the bar. It's past midnight, Friday. Here comes the Bride. The storm blew out, and now the air's flat as warm beer. Miami is a morgue. Literally. Hearses all over. Ambulance sirens day and night. Old people coming out of the woodwork. Once I told Sam, "Let's get out of Miami. Let's go to L.A. or Dallas."

But he's set at the *Herald*.

"And our people are here," he said.

"I'm your people now," I said. "You're mine."

"Diana, we belong to families," he said. "We have histories."

"Water over the dam."

"The well from which we drink."

I should know better than to fight him with words. He's the writer.

There's Wayne. I see him through the rippled red glass window. He's on fire. Burning up behind the bar. He's pouring beer: It looks like lava. Where else would Wayne Cutler work, but a place that looks like the inside of a volcano?

In I walk.

FLORENCE

SHE SHOULD HAVE taken the whole week off, I told her. Not just two days. She's never been a help to me. But before her own wedding. You'd think it would be a time for pitching in. Doing her share without being asked. Not her. Eleven A.M. on Thursday and she wasn't even dressed.

"What exactly needs to be done?" she said. "It's not like we're having a hundred people."

"We're having what we can afford," I said.

Immediate family, minus a few. No one from my side. All I have is my sister Catherine, in Cleveland,

and her husband Jim's just a week out of open-heart surgery. Then, of course, my ex-husband, Karl, and his brother don't speak, so Justin wasn't invited.

But no matter how small, a wedding is work.

"Details mount up, Diana. Which you'd know, if you cared to involve yourself. And turn that thing off, I can't stand the noise anymore."

She uses that blow dryer like it was oxygen. Every time I turn around, she's wetting her head under the faucet, or taking a shower, giving herself a new hairdo. On her looks she'll spend hours. Pays a fortune for makeup. Her room's like a movie star's dressing room. You can't even see the top of her bureau for all the bottles and jars and tubes. Hours at it. But will she do one thing more in this apartment than I absolutely require? Never.

"Make me out a list," she said.

She pulled her fingers through her thick yellow hair, and it looked like honey pouring down her hands. When she was two, she was still newborn bald. I thought she'd never have a full head. Nothing worked out the way I imagined. What I worried over turned out fine. What I hoped for failed me.

"What good's a list if you're loafing?"

"I still have a lot of time left in the day," she said.

"If you get yourself out of this room and dressed, you might."

This is Diana Fry: She turned that dryer to top speed and aimed it at me like a gun.

"I know," she said. "I'm a regular criminal. First-

[148   ]

degree laziness. Lock me up for twenty years and throw away—"

"Oh make sense," I said, turning to leave. "Will you please."

In the kitchen I wrote out the list:

1. Call the organist (Mrs. Jessup) and make sure she has the sheet music for "True Love."

2. Pick up the corsages at Pape's Flower Shop and put them in the refrigerator. White lily for you. Pink orchids for me, Charlotte, Mary, your grandmother and Mrs. Cortez. Check the ribbons—are they frayed? Are the pins in right?

3. Check with Brewster about the folding chairs at the reception. Make sure he doesn't give us any scratched ones. (Brewster is the janitor at Holy Redeemer, if you remember.)

4. Decide on napkins, once and for all. White or pink? This is the final time.

5. Film. Get three rolls for the Brownie. I don't like depending on your father for pictures, even if he said he'd take them.

I leaned the note against the wheat-germ jar. Sam has her eating right, another thing I never could accomplish.

"Diana," I told her, "I'm going now. The note's in the kitchen."

But I'm not sure she even heard me through the door and the racket of the dryer. Sometimes I think everything in the world was invented to keep me from communicating with my own child.

But I didn't have time to brood. I had things to do myself. First I had to pick up my dress for the wedding. It needed alteration. I had them close the slits up each side of the skirt. The neckline was too low; I had them put an insert there. I don't believe in display.

"How come you bought a dress you don't really like?" Diana said. "You're changing the whole style."

"I got a good buy on it," I said. "And there's not much to choose from, if I'm limited to purple."

"Lavender."

"Same thing. I'm too sallow for purples, but you were determined."

"It's my wedding," she said. "And Sam's mother—"

"Diana, don't let me know there's one more person in the world I have to accommodate myself to. If that's the case, don't tell me about it."

"She's had this silk for years and—"

"And so I have to buy a purple dress. Well, don't criticize my choice. At least spare me that."

I would never tell her where I bought it. Second Time Around. Everything they sell is used. I don't believe in buying new, other than uniforms. People spoil themselves. Even the saleslady was uncomfortable when I said I wanted a dress for my daughter's wedding.

"I know you get some evening clothes in now and then," I said.

"But for a wedding—"

"A wedding," I said, "lasts for a few hours and no one looks at anyone but the bride."

"Oh," she said, "but your own daughter's—"

I was already on my way to the fitting room. Working in a hospital teaches you: From the time you're born, you get old and shabby, patching holes, replacing parts, finally wearing out and dying. All the new clothes in the world don't change those facts. Why pretend?

"But it has a stain at the hem," the saleslady said when I brought her the dress I'd chosen.

"Anyone looking at my hem has his eyes in the wrong place," I said. "What exactly is the tax on twenty-five dollars?"

Once I saw they were set on this, Diana and Sam, I called up his mother. This was months ago. I know what's proper.

"Would you care to come for lunch?" I asked her. "Monday is my day off."

"Sí," she said.

Like I was foreigner, too. They forget where they are sometimes. So many of them move up here, they think they're still in their own country. You're the one feels strange, not knowing Spanish. A lot of them live in my building. Just smelling their food, I get heartburn. I don't hold it against them. It's all they know. You'd think they'd try to become more American. But they don't. People are stubborn.

I fixed tuna fish on romaine lettuce, with fruited Jell-O salad on the side. I don't go in for spice. If she expected hot sauce and chili peppers, she'd come to the wrong place. You have to draw the line. You can't spend your whole life pleasing others. You can't cater to their every whim. You have to draw the line.

At noon on the dot the doorbell buzzed. We have a speaker system in our building, for security. You can never be too safe.

"Yes," I said, into the speaker box on the kitchen wall, beside the phone.

She said, "I am Maria Elena Cortez."

You would have thought she was someone special, the way she said her name. You would have thought she was famous.

"Come right up," I said.

I pressed the button that unlocked the lobby door for her. Diana always says, "This building is like a fortress." I would hope so. She's the one with all the so-called experience. But you'd think she never heard of crime. Walks the streets at night like muggers don't exist. Never locks her car. I bought her one of those whistles once and a can of mace, but does she carry them with her? No. "Just because *you're* paranoid doesn't mean *I* have to be," she'll say. Some remark like that.

Mrs. Cortez was dressed to the hilt. I was in my seersucker shirtwaist; she had on white pants and a blazing orange top, silk if I wasn't mistaken. I wore my Red Cross wedgies. She had black patent leather high-heeled sandals on her feet. Painted toenails. Lots of gold chains around her neck. I was surprised to see the wedding ring. She didn't come to America with her husband, I know that much. "He stayed behind," is how Sam describes it. I can figure that out. I know all about that. Don't I? Four years later and she's still waiting for him to join her. Keeping herself young for him. Some women never learn. Her jet black hair was sleeked back into a bun. Where was the gray? A woman with a grown son has to have a few gray hairs. And her face. Smooth as teak wood. I could tell: She'd had a face-lift. What some women will go through. Thousands of dollars. For weeks afterwards, you're swollen and bruised. And a few years later, you have to endure it again. For what? I look my age. When I face the mirror, I see who I am. I have nothing to hide.

"So," she said, perched like a tropical bird on my sofa. "The children have decided to marry."

She wasn't any happier about it than I was.

But she had airs.

From the way she was looking over the apartment, I could tell she wouldn't choose Diana for her son. He has a college degree and writes articles for the Miami *Herald*. He needs a serious-minded girl: I knew she was thinking that.

"I hope you like tuna," I said. "Because that's what we have."

Right in the middle of our silent lunch, she put her fork down on her plate. She turned her palms to the ceiling, then she brought them down to the table. "What can I do?" she said. "I think it's wrong."

Her hands were old. They can fix everything, but they can't fix hands.

"I'm for it," I said, but only because I knew she wasn't.

I admit it: when Diana told me Sam Cortez had asked her to marry him, I thought, I have to warn him off. My own daughter. But there's no point prettying it up.

The day Karl left she turned on me, and she's been nothing but trouble since. I kept thinking it would run its course. But her resentment turned out to be endless. How could she blame me, when he was the one who left?

"If we had a boy," Karl said, "I'd be getting the brunt of it. That's how it works, I'm afraid."

In that calm voice. Like he was explaining tooth decay, or why the bathroom faucet dripped.

I screamed, " 'Don't talk to me like I'm stupid!' "

But that wasn't what I meant. I meant: *I want this to be as hard on you as it is on me.*

Then she started running around. Before it had just been back talk. Now the truant officer was looking for me at work three, four times a month. Teachers called me up at the hospital or at home at night. Then she met Wayne Cutler and she wasn't coming home at all. I was losing my mind over it.

Karl said, "I'll take her. Maybe Charlotte and I can help her to—"

"You've done enough! I'd never allow you to have her!"

He didn't press. If he'd pressed, I might have agreed. But you can always count on Karl Fry to back off.

Except when it came to leaving us. Who would have imagined him capable? In Washington, I never understood how he functioned at work. "I write guidelines," he'd say when you asked him what he did there. Guidelines? A man who'd take all day to fix a leaky faucet and wind up bungling the job? A man who never learned to read a map? I kept expecting him to forget halfway through packing why he was putting his belongings into suitcases and cardboard boxes. He would stare at the socks in his hands. Balled up neatly like I did. Or the pile of T-shirts, folded as even as a stack of envelopes. *Where am I going?* he would think. *Did I apply for a transfer? Is the agency sending me to the Wharton School of Finance after all?*

Nothing would explain his confusion. Carefully, he'd put everything back in his dresser and desk.

"Florence," he'd ask me at supper (I would be fixing stuffed peppers, which he liked), "Florence, were we planning a vacation for tomorrow?"

I'd say, "Of course not, it's not even summer."

I'd go on serving the food. He would look at me blankly. We would never mention his leaving again. It would be one more strange thing about him for me to live with.

But he finished the job. He never lost sight of his goal. He wasn't at all confused about that, or even unsteady. By evening he was gone. It took Diana three days to understand.

"You mean permanent," she said. "For good."

"For good," I said; and here is what I think. I think she decided it was my saying it that made it true, not his going. Like I held the rope.

Well. Maybe I did. Maybe I could have changed his mind, wooed him back. The truth is, I never wanted him back. I hated him for leaving, but I never, not once, wanted him back.

This is how it was at the beginning.

Our first place was a three-room furnished apartment over top a beauty parlor. Dottie and Lil's Hair Salon. You could smell permanent wave solution in our place all the time. Everything I cooked tasted like shampoo. I have to admit it: we didn't mind. We kept a can of room deodorant spray, Spring Garden scent, in every room. We laughed about it. Young people are fools. One day I brought home surgical masks—I was in nursing school then, Columbia Hospital for Women is where I trained—and I wrote my name on one mask, Karl's on the other. I inked on flowers and hearts. I set them on our plates like napkins. Karl got home usual time. He laughed himself to tears. We wore them while we washed the dishes.

He worked for the U.S. Department of Labor, G.S. 5. Mostly, he clipped newspapers. Anything to do with unions. I made out like he was a Presidential aide.

"I know you'll go far," I used to say. "You have drive."

He had nothing of the sort. I thought telling him he did would make it true. I thought marriage was one long audition. Each person trying out all his or her life for the role the other person wrote all the lines for. Once Karl said, "Florence, I wish you'd just relax and be yourself," and I thought, *You don't wish anything of the kind.*

I know how it is with Diana and Sam. She's pretending to the hilt. Him, too. They don't know it yet, but they will.

"He brings out my good qualities," she tells me. "Whether you think I have any or not."

A nice girl is a nice girl, period. No matter who

she's with. A nice girl isn't snippy when it suits her. One day Sam will wake up and realize Diana never was the wife he had in mind. She'll have a morning like that herself, about him. Everybody does.

I told Karl, "So you're disappointed. I'm not what you hoped for. Well, you think you're a prize? You're not. Not anywhere near. But I know my responsibilities. I know what's expected of me. I believe in duty. Whatever happened to—"

He cut me off. "Florence, I'm too lonely here."

That's Karl. Always changing the topic. You can never have a normal conversation with him. It's a wonder I didn't go mad, all the years I lived with that man.

They're crazy, the Frys, the whole lot of them.

I wanted to change my name back to Langley after the divorce. But then Diana was a Fry and it would have been one more confusion. What I did was get as far away from them as possible. Came down here to Miami where my sister Catherine was. When what happens after a year but her husband James takes a job in Cleveland and I'm left by myself among strangers.

You can't depend on a soul.

But I was learning to make my own way.

I had the job at St. Joseph's my third week down. Cardiology. Catherine helped me find a nice apartment on a bus line. When I signed the lease, I remember thinking: *Who'd believe I'd ever wind up in Miami, living in a pink building with palm trees out front and a swimming pool on the roof?*

I said to Catherine, "This isn't one of those singles places now, Catherine, is it?"

And she told me, "Florence, things are more colorful down here, that's all. It's just the decor."

I'm partial to neutral tones. In Washington, I always liked late autumn best, after all the leaves were gone. Black trees, pale skies, the sun far away and milky. It calmed me. I had to give that up in Florida, but at least I was hundreds of miles from the Frys.

Or so I thought. You can't count on anything. Nine months after Catherine leaves, who appears on my ward one Saturday, waiting for me at the nurses' station, but Karl.

My first thought was: *What's he doing here early? I don't get off my shift for another fifteen minutes.*

We had lived together as man and wife for thirteen years. In Washington, he'd always picked me up weekends when I worked at Holy Cross. Then I remembered where I was. What had happened to my life. I felt like one of my patients whose medication has worn off early.

"What are you doing here?" I said. I could hardly breathe from the pain.

"Florence," he said.

Like that was an answer. Like knowing my name gave him permission to be on the other side of the desk, no more than two feet away from me.

"Answer my question, Karl," I said. I made myself listen to the page: "Dr. Brady, stat. Dr. Newcomb, come to the nurses' station on Pediatrics. Dr. Jiminez, stat." I watched the lights blinking on the call board. Room 16A. Room 22B. A hospital makes sense. People know what's expected of them. Sick or healthy, they know how they're supposed to feel.

"Florence," he said. "I've come here to live. I've moved down. I need to be closer to Diana, you see. Involved in her life."

All I could think was: *Get me an empty bed, I am going to have a collapse.* Not that I did. At least not in a way that was noticeable to anyone. I kept on at my job. I did the grocery shopping. I fixed meals, did laundry; I made Diana do her homework every night and not with that rock music blaring either. Thursday evenings Karl rode the bus from Collins Avenue, where he was living in a boarding house. I would go directly to my room. When I heard Diana shut the door behind her, I would fall asleep. Falling it was. Sometimes I would jerk so, I'd come close to rolling off the bed. I learned to hold on to the headboard as soon as I lay down, so as not to have that jolt. I wouldn't wake until he brought Diana home, about nine or so, and then I'd be in a daze until I got her off to sleep. Until I could resume my own.

This went on for six months, these lost Thursdays. Then one evening when Diana was gone, instead of heading for the bedroom, I made myself a cup of Postum and sat on the stool at the pass-through bar that divided the kitchen from the pine-paneled dining area. I could see the sun dissolving, a red strip in the sky. I stared and stared at that strip. It turned into a person. At least it looked like a person to me. A person face down on a bed, getting weaker and weaker, all but disappearing. Then I realized: That was me. I had fallen down inside myself the day Karl announced he was back in our lives again. Oh, it tore me up to realize how I'd faded. For the next three hours, I cried like a baby. When I heard Diana on the stairs, I went to bed so she wouldn't see me broken down. After that, I got used to his living near us. The day he married Charlotte, I bought myself a steak and two new uniforms.

You can get through anything in life, as long as you don't count on being happy.

I started out with the same dreams as any girl. Sure I did. Diana's jaw would drop if she could see me young. All the time I spent doing my hair with those metal curlers we had. Giving myself manicures. Making nice clothes. I liked nice clothes. I would go to the remnant box in the yard goods section in Kresge's Five and Ten, and find a piece of paisley print cotton, some seersucker, enough corduroy for a jumper or matching skirts for Catherine and me. My mother called me "Miss America." My father said, "We're going to see this girl on magazine covers someday. You can mark it down." Catherine didn't care about looks the way I did. She said she didn't have the patience for it.

I said, "Do you want to wind up a spinster?"

But look how things turned out. She's been happy with James for twenty years, and I'm the one getting old by myself.

We lived in College Park, on account of Dad's job. He taught in agriculture school. He wrote a book on herbicides, which he approved of and Mother didn't. She being a nurse and concerned about health. It wasn't all they disagreed about. I don't know how old I was when I understood why she cried so much. He was a ladies' man.

I knew it and I didn't. But I knew. I started noticing how he teased the waitress when we went to a restaurant. Once I surprised him in his office on campus. Opened the door without knocking. He was there with a student, not much older than me, and I saw him let go of her hand like it had burned him. All the color went out of his face. I pretended not to notice anything. I had my visit with him and then I went home. Mother was making Apple Betty and listening to "One Man's Family" on the radio. She didn't work while we were growing up. But she subscribed to *Nursing Today* and had her own blood-pressure kit.

On Saturday afternoons, in my teenage years, I would walk up and down the street and count how many boys looked at me "that way." The way my father looked at waitresses, or that student whose hand he was holding in his office. The way—why not say it?—he looked at me and Catherine.

So I counted those boys. There were plenty of them. But I didn't like them. Those looks. I never said so, hardly even to myself. But more and more I hardened to those winks and stares; my smile grew phony and stiff. When I ask myself what it was about Karl that got to me, it was that he didn't look at me "that way" when he looked. His eyes weren't like pincers. His mouth wasn't hungry. He said, "Excuse me, but I would like to buy you a Coca-Cola." It went to my head. I took it for self-confidence, that invitation to a stranger.

It went to my head. How could I have known he just needed someone to take care of him, and his mother was losing the patience for it. Dad picked it up right away, but I wasn't much for listening to his ideas about anything.

"Nice enough boy," he said. "But soft. A little confused, even."

Mother gave Dad a hard look.

"Florence has found herself a gentleman," she said.

As if good manners told her everything she needed to know about Karl Fry.

Well, I wish she'd been alive when he came into our bedroom one night and informed me, oh so politely, that he was leaving.

"There's no love in this house, Florence" is what he said.

Like we were out of milk. He said it like that. After the years I'd catered to his strange habits, his silences, his fits of weeping over the silliest things. A grown man, weeping. It made my skin crawl sometimes. Then I'd think, *Well, at least he isn't a bully like his brother, Justin.* Neither of them are normal.

And then he ups and leaves. You can't depend on a soul.

I remember the first time I met all the Frys together. It was the summer I graduated from high school. Karl and I were "going steady" now. He had given me a wristwatch, an Elgin. Lord knows how he managed to save up for it.

"Give it back," Dad said. "That's as good as an engagement ring. You're too young for that. Besides, the boy's not . . . right."

What did I know? He was a college boy. I used that like my mother used good manners. I made it count for everything. You can pretty up anything, if you want to feel a certain way about it. I wore the watch day and night. I wore it for years. Then one day I lost it. By then I hardly cared.

But the night I met the Frys, I cared. I wanted to make a good impression. I wanted them to like me. Going to meet Karl's family was like trying out for a play, or applying for membership in an exclusive club. How did I know the play would bomb, the club would fold, I'd be thirty-three and no better off than the day I met him? I should have known it was trouble when we got to Karl's apartment door. Rose swung it open to greet us. She hugged and kissed me like I was a long-lost relative. It was written all over her: *Take him off my hands.*

I didn't pick up on that. Then the smells. She had three different meals cooking at once in the kitchen. I had gone in to help her serve. Karl liked liver and onions, so that was simmering on one burner. Justin's spaghetti sauce bubbled on another. A pot of stew on a third, for Wendell. We ladies can have a bit of each, she said. She winked at me like we were in the same secret club. She saw my puzzlement. "I could never please them altogether," she said. "Someone was always sulking, ruining it for the rest. Finally I said, 'All right, I'll do it like a diner, that way there won't be any complaints all through the meal.' I guess you could say I spoiled them some."

Right then I should have understood. The way those odors crashed into each other. The confusion in the kitchen. And then the table: everyone with their separate food, no sharing, no "pass the peas" even. They might as well have been in separate rooms. Or just like Rose said: strangers in the same diner, ordering from Rose's menu, nothing more in common than that. They didn't even look related. Wendell was stiff and thin and yellowed as a pencil with an eraser-bald head; he squinted like a man with a perpetual headache; he examined his food like he was searching for evidence. He chewed carefully, waiting for the sliver of glass.

"What did you think of my father?" Karl would ask me later.

"Very dignified," I said. Of Justin I would say, "Full of life." How did I arrive at that error? Easily. He was a younger version of Robert Preston in *The Music Man*—conning everyone blind with that practiced grin. *Full of mischief* was what I should have said; *full of lies.* And Karl. I mistook him for comforting but Dad was right: Soft is soft. Jell-O, custard, nothing substantial. And then he ups and leaves. You'd think he was a prize I'd never appreciated, instead of a lemon I'd learned to put up with.

When I met Charlotte, I thought: *She's the way I was at the beginning with him. Behaves like a girl.*

I'm past all that.

Just let me get Diana settled down and I won't have to take my Valium anymore. I'll just have myself to think about. I'll finally have life whittled down to where I can handle it.

I had Diana in the dead of winter. December 14, 1962. When we moved down here, she was ten. It seems she hasn't had a real birthday since. Where's the snow? The roads were so bad, our Plymouth skidded all the way to the hospital. At one red light, we couldn't stop at all.

"You'll kill us both!" I screamed.

Karl said, "We're fine, we're both just fine."

I hadn't meant him at all. I realized that. I'd meant the baby and me. Truth comes on you like that. Accidentally. I see it all the time on the ward. The things people say when they're in pain, or scared, or so tired they drop their guard. You can always tell when people have spoken the truth: They look ashamed.

Tell me this isn't my life.

Tell me this isn't happening to my life.

Tell me these policeman aren't standing in my living room. This is a dream. I'm dreaming this whole thing.

"Apparently he's got a gun," the short one says. "This Wayne Cutler. Apparently he's got a gun and he's holding her hostage there. In one of the cabins at her father's place."

The tall one says, "There doesn't seem to be a ransom involved, Mrs. Fry. We seem to be dealing with a lover's quarrel or something of that nature."

"She's getting married tomorrow," I tell them. "To Sam Cortez. She doesn't see Wayne Cutler anymore. This is a terrible mistake."

The tall one says, "Might be terrible, but it's no mistake. That's why we're here."

He looks just like a patient I have on the ward. Old man on a respirator.

"I know your father," I say. "He'll pull through."

"You know my—? He's been dead for years, Mrs. Fry." They give each other strange looks. "Mrs. Fry. If you could sit down. We need to ask some questions here."

It's two o'clock in the morning. My hair's up in sponge rollers. I've got night cream all over my face. You wouldn't think you'd be worried about how you look when you're half in shock, but that's how it is. People are small, they really are. I see it all the time in the hospital. Ladies primping for the doctor who's going to tell them if their husbands are alive or dead. Grown men fixing their ties and slicking down their hair when a nurse comes in with a pain pill for their wives just back from OR.

"You want me to sit down?" I say.

I perch on the end of the blue tub chair, the officers sit on the sofa. The floral slipcover shrank when I washed it. Even though I did it by hand in cold water and hung it over the tub to dry. The old green upholstery shows through near the legs. I feel I should apologize for it. For the way I look. For everything that isn't right in this apartment.

"I'm sorry."

"Sorry?"

The tall one's got his pencil ready, like I'm going to give him a confession.

I sweep my hand from my hair rollers to the sofa to the dirty dishes in the kitchen sink they haven't even seen yet. All around. I try to cover all the mistakes. All the failures.

"I tried!" I tell them. I'm tearing up now. "God knows I tried!"

Now I'm really crying. The night cream turns to liquid and drips on my robe. But I don't care. I don't care anymore. I'll tell them the whole story. What's the point of keeping up appearances anymore? Two policemen are standing in my house in the middle of the night. Policemen. I have never gotten a traffic ticket; I have never cheated on my taxes; I have never taken packs of sugar from restaurants or towels from hotels. All my life I've been so careful! How could I know what to do with a daughter who was taking chances even in her crib? I tried to teach her to protect herself. But she got more and more brazen.

"Mrs. Fry, if you could answer some questions—"

But I've started the story. It's pouring out of me like blood. "And we couldn't keep her in her crib. She'd climb out and wander the house while we were asleep. Once I heard this crash and I charged downstairs with a lamp in my hand to use on the robber's head. But what do I find? In the dark? My year-old baby's knocked over my figurine of the Blessed Mother. It's in pieces all over the dining room floor. I told Karl we had to put

[167   ]

netting over the crib, or—this I read in *Ladies' Home Journal*—a screen door on her room we'd lock from the outside. He wouldn't hear of it.

" 'You'd be creating a prison, Florence,' he said.

"I asked him what exactly he suggested.

" 'I suggest we have shifts,' he said, 'and when she climbs out, we put her back in, over and over, until she learns it isn't acceptable behavior.'

"I said, 'Shifts? We couldn't wait until night feedings were over so we could get our proper rest again. Now you want us back on shifts?'

"He said, 'Florence, we are parents now.'

"He always set it up like I was the selfish one. I came to believe it for a time. You live with a man like that long enough, his ideas seep into you like wood rot."

"Mrs. Fry—"

"I should have taken my name back after the divorce, and changed Diana's, too. I should have done a lot of things differently. I know that. But I had Karl to contend with. And his mother. She's a meddler, Rose Fry. When I was still married and living in Washington, she was always calling. Coming over on the bus even though she had to transfer twice. And turning Diana against me. I'd say, 'Diana, you have to clean your room before supper,' and Rose would say, 'Let her play cards with her granny, Florence. I'll help her tidy up before she goes to bed.' And she'd deal out two hands of Old Maid like I'd given permission, which I had not. Things like that happen often enough, and they did, a child gets a message: *Ignore your mother; I'm more fun.*

" 'If you would soften up some, Florence,' Karl

would say when I'd complain. 'If you'd have some fun yourself with Diana—'

"Well, I am not a fun type. I'm an organizer is what I am. That's how I contribute. People need order in their lives, don't they? Meals on time, things in their proper places, rules that tell them what they can and cannot do. Don't they?

"I couldn't get any of that to stick with Diana. I'd say, 'Set the table,' and she'd put the forks on the wrong side of the plates and forget the knives. Or else she'd fill the water glasses so high, they'd spill on your shirt when you lifted one to drink. I used to think she did things like that on purpose, but after a while I could see she just didn't care. She'd never learned what I'd tried to teach her. She tuned me out when I talked. Let her grandmother tell her a story and she'd hang on every word. That child's tongue would dangle like a hungry pup for whatever Rose had to say. I'd open my mouth and her eyelids would droop. She'd stifle a yawn. Nothing got through.

"And then, of course, her uncle was off getting himself arrested and in the newspapers. Setting a terrible example. We'd turn on the news and there he'd be, leading a demonstration, standing up at the podium and screaming about imperialists and Ho Chi Minh and all those hippies cheering him on like he was a movie star. Diana loved Justin, of course. He'd come by sometimes when he and Karl were still on terms. Justin would do magic tricks for Diana and sing her flirty songs. I'd see her smile like a woman. This when she was seven, eight.

" 'Bar him from the house!' I told Karl. 'I don't care if he is your brother, I don't want him here. Next thing you know he'll be giving her drugs.'

"And the neighbors talking. I had to deal with that, too.

" 'Isn't your brother-in-law Justin Fry?' they'd say. 'Why doesn't he move to Cuba?' I'd die a thousand deaths.

" 'He's just crazy,' I'd say, like that was better than being against your own government. Here his father works for the F.B.I. and his brother's at Labor, and Justin Fry is running around the country for the communists. And my daughter thinks he's wonderful. Don't think he didn't have an influence. Don't think he doesn't bear some responsibility for where she is right now!"

It hits me full force. Where she is right now.

"Oh my God!" I'm screaming. "He'll hurt my girl!"

The tall one's got me by one arm and the short one by the other. I can't tell if I'm being arrested, kidnapped or rescued.

"Help me!" I'm yelling. "Help me and my girl!"

I told Diana the first time I met Wayne Cutler that he was no good.

"I'm not looking for good," she said. "I'm looking for fun."

Well, she's having fun now, isn't she. The night before her wedding. We are all having the times of our lives tonight. And Sam. That nice boy. The hopes he built on her, the plans he made. I should have warned him off. I should have joined up with his mother and said, "Diana is just not the right girl for you." But I started believing that things might work out. At least as well as they do for any of us. She had a chance. And she throws it all away on Wayne Cutler.

I'd ask her and ask her, "Where's your self-respect?"

"I guess I left it in D.C. Maybe you sold it at the yard sale you had before you made us move."

"Can't you be nasty and mean," I'd say.

"Can't I."

From down the road, Karl's place looks like a carnival's camped there.

Closer up, it looks like a war.

Or prison, after an escape. Except here the criminal's broken in instead of out. Just like a TV program. Once I pulled myself together in the apartment, this all started to seem like a TV program to me. If I reached out to touch anything there, I knew I'd come up against a sheet of glass exactly like the screen on my RCA. The officers ask me questions, but I don't bother to answer. They couldn't hear me, anyhow. They're part of the show. Everybody but me is part of the show. I'm all alone, watching, trying to stay awake.

I've never been inside their house before. Karl's and Charlotte's. Fry's Lodge. They live in the main house and rent out the cottages. They just make ends meet. What with the guests to care for, and her own retarded daughter, and Karl, Charlotte must work like a dog. If I had to pick Diana up there, I blew the horn and waited in the car. Not that I did that often. Getting her back and forth was Karl's job. I told him, "You wanted the divorce. You decided to move here. You do the running around." But things came up. Their Chevy would break down. Or Charlotte would be laid up with flu—he waits on her hand and foot even when she's fine. So what was I going to do? Refuse to get Diana or drop her there? Give them reason to judge me selfish? No. As it is, they have always treated me like a dried-up spinster. Maybe Karl has amnesia. Maybe he doesn't remember that I was married to him for thirteen years and gave birth to his child. Raised her myself, too, for all practical purposes. Even when he was there, he wasn't. Head in the clouds, that's him. Lived in another world. And then he tells me, "There's no love in this house, Florence." No husband and no father would have been more to the point. I could never depend on him and neither could Diana. And look what's become of us.

I never noticed how run-down this place was before. All lit up, I can see how shabby it is. Shingles missing on the roof. An upstairs shutter dangling from a bolt. The siding needs paint so bad it's practically back to the natural wood in spots. I never noticed all this disrepair before. Now it's all I see. All those years I suffered from the thought that someone else had brought Karl around, made him responsible in a way I couldn't. Now I know he's the same neglectful, sloppy, clumsy man he always was. This house is proof: He's the same with Charlotte as he was with me.

He's at the door when we walk up. Me and the police. He sees me and shakes his head, no, no, like he does. He gets those tears in his eyes, like always. I want to be numb. Not be anything but tired. But he's making me sick to my stomach. I'm so close to him I can see the mole on his cheek. Then I'm inside. Oh, I am so sick! Charlotte's body is real, real! Mary's breasts show through her nightgown! The smells! Rose!

"I need some water," I tell Charlotte. "I'm feeling sick."

In the front hall, there's a coat tree I lean against. I turn into a scarecrow. Karl's hands flutter around me like birds.

"This is a horror, Florence."

His voice is ragged. Each word gets torn up before it gets out of his mouth. I stare at him. When Charlotte comes with the water, I hold the glass with two hands to keep it steady. Even so, some spills down my dress.

That they should see me like this!

"You blame me," I say. "I can see it on your faces. You think this is my fault."

Charlotte says, "Nobody blames—"

"You do!" I yell. "You think I raised her wrong!"

"Florence," Karl says.

He puts his hands out to me like the Pope giving blessings.

"And I don't need forgiveness either, because I did the best I could! I did the best I could and there was nobody to help me and I don't need you to—"

And then we hear it. Like popping a paper bag after you blow air into it.

"Get down!" the policeman hollers. "Down!"

And we collapse on the floor; we go down like people who have just been shot. Maybe we have. Maybe the pain will come in a minute. Maybe we're already dead. Oh please, oh please, oh please, let us already be dead.

KARL

"Your daughter is out of danger," the doctor says.

He is showing us an X ray, a dark spot beneath her shoulder where the bullet lodged.

"The surgery was entirely successful. Her vital signs are strong. We'll have her out of Intensive Care in a day or two."

Without complications.

He is talking to a father and mother who lived apart even in the years they shared the same house or slept beside each other in the bed in which their daughter was conceived. We are the wound our child bears.

When I met Charlotte, I told her, "Diana won't forgive me for the divorce."

Charlotte said, "She can't forgive you until you forgive yourself."

"Have you forgiven *your*self?" I said. "For *your* divorce?"

She smiled. Pain gathered in her eyes. "Every day," she said. "Every single day."

"We are very grateful for all you've done," I tell the doctor.

Florence bunches together the shreds of tissue in her lap.

"Don't say 'we.' "

She refuses to look at me. "I don't want him to think we're related."

Without complications, doctor? You do not seem to recognize the symptoms before you.

"You—that is, each of you—can see her, for a few minutes now. She'll be groggy still, from the anesthesia. Don't be alarmed if she doesn't know you. We expect a certain disorientation for a day or so."

"I'm going first," Florence says.

She stands up, wavering like a woman who's had too much to drink. Pieces of tissue float to the floor.

"I'll get that, Florence,"

I bend to clean up the litter, but she pushes me away. It is the first time since we have been divorced that she has touched me in any way.

"No favors!" she says. Her voice is thin, a ghost of her true voice. "No favors!"

Then she is on her knees, plucking tissue from the plush rug.

While she visits Diana I sit in the waiting room between my mother and Charlotte, my hands in theirs. Sam paces the stretch of corridor between this pod of couches and the nurses' station fifteen feet away. Like some parody of the wedding that never took place—the immediate family assembled, the groom ready, the bride not yet visible—we each ask: How did this happen? How could this have happened to us?

We each have our own stories.

Mine is no more true than Mother's or Florence's or Diana's. Sam has his. If my brother were here, he would assemble his own memories, his own grievances, his own guilts, his own explanations.

If we all had the courage to tell our stories to one another, and the courage to listen, we might heal ourselves, each of us wounded as we are, each of us needing intensive care.

When Florence returns from her third visit to Diana— we are each allowed five minutes every hour—my mother says, "Karl, I'd like to go this time in your place, if I could."

"Immediate family," Florence says. "They only want immediate family. That's me and Karl and Sam because he's the husband less a day."

"I think Diana would be very happy for you to be with her, Mother," I say. "I'll tell the nurse you'll go instead of me."

As we rise Florence makes fists of her hands and her knuckles turn white. Sam touches her shoulder. "Florence," he says, "if you could put your anger—"

"Whose side are you on?" she says. Her words are a hiss through fused teeth. But she does not try to bar us from passing. She does not even seem to realize that we have walked away.

I tell the nurse stationed outside the Intensive Care ward that Mother will visit Diana in my place this hour. The nurse hands her a plastic pass.

Mother says, "I want to look nice for her. My eyes are so puffy."

She takes out her compact and powders the pouches beneath her lashes. She smoothes her skirt.

"Prepare yourself," I tell her. "She's lost blood. She has tubes and wires everywhere. She's—"

"She's my beautiful little girl," Mother says. She smiles. "She's my precious child."

In she walks.

I remember thinking at the airport: *She looks old, my mother.*

As if in the last year, ten had crowded into her face. Last spring I took Charlotte and Mary to Washington at cherry blossom time and we stayed with Mother in the apartment where I was raised. Raised I was. Like the begonias she tended on the windowsill in the kitchen. Lovingly, but with an eye out for rot.

"Well, Mother," I said when we arrived at the Lodge, "what do you think of our place?"

"Beautiful," she said. "Surely impressive."

But she moved with the smallest of steps, as if she were in retreat even as her shoes carried her forward, toward the house. When I was a boy, she would tell me often how handsome I was, and I would observe her body strain against the lie she believed I required.

Years back, when she came down to nurse me after my operation, I told her, "Mother, please, I am a grown man. I do not need you to baby me like this."

Her eyes clouded. "Then what did I come here for?"

She learned belligerence from my father, though hers is a weak imitation.

"I would like us to be friends," I said. "I would like us to get to know each other as friends."

"Friends you can get in the Rotary Club," she said. "Mothers come one to a customer."

She is a woman in strong need of a friend. She was never close to anyone but Father, and that was not a congenial affair. We lived in an apartment, and although they always argued in their bedroom behind a locked door, Justin and I heard every accusation, every threat, every statement of remorse. Justin laughed when my parents fought. At first I took it for the embarrassed laughter of a child witnessing an accident who masks his terror with smiles of shame. But Justin's glee was not that kind. For him the battles between our father and mother were sports events he came to enjoy in the way some men take to boxing matches and hockey players whacking each other with their sticks. I cried when our parents argued.

"You're just like a girl," Justin would say. "Sissy. Why don't you give up and buy a dress?"

My mother would tell me, "Now, Karl, that's the way your father and I communicate. We don't mean each other harm." I struggled to believe it, in their marriage, in my own. I heard my parents' arguments piped through my voice and Florence's. When a door slammed, two resounded. Finally I said, "Florence, there is no love in this home."

I spoke in sorrow, in confession, but she took it as indictment.

After the divorce, I told her, "Florence, I hope we can be friends."

But she said, "I hate you, I will always hate you."

That was years ago, but to this day we speak indirectly, through Diana. When it was time to plan the wedding, Florence used Charlotte as a go-between, discussing the plans with her rather than me, deciding with her on food and flowers and such.

"There she is," I said to Mother as we approached the house. Charlotte was framed in the doorway.

Sweat-polished, air-conditioning on the blink again, top-knot half undone, perspiration staining her light blue sundress dark under the arms and down the front in streaks as if a child might have stolen up on her with a paintbrush, yet how cool she seemed, unflustered and calm, immune to the inescapable heat.

"Rose," Charlotte said, "it is so good to have you here!" and her arms stretched forward in welcome.

Mother paused for a moment, halted completely,

as if making a decision about whether to move forward or turn back. Mary tugged on Mother's pocketbook, her childish grin nearly a grimace, so hard was she working to charm this relation of mine. I, myself, placed a hand on Mother's shoulder and felt her soften under my touch.

"It's so good to be here," she said finally, trying to mean it, and released herself into Charlotte's embrace.

Not until then did I realize that at the airport Mother and I had not greeted each other with our customary hug. Instead, we had offered tentative pecks on the cheek, bending towards each other while maintaining enough distance for a third person to stand between us. Now that space filled with feature, form: Justin's absence, vivid as a photographic negative, followed us into the house.

While I took her bags upstairs, I imagined the scene as it would materialize. She would bring it up at dinner.

"Karl," she would say, and pause, as if my name were rebuke enough, as if it carried within it a lifetime of disappointments for her.

"Karl, will you please tell me why Justin has not been invited."

By then her voice would be emptied of anger, and she would speak in the same tone one might use to ask for the time. But I would notice the way she cut her meat, the precise ferocity of her knife strokes.

"Mother," I would say, "we simply do not get along."

"Simply" being a euphemism for the complexity

of estrangement. Love is straightforward. We are wrong to call it mystery. When two people love each other, their feeling reveals itself in every detail of their relation. Even clandestine love asserts itself, demands light and the breathing of ordinary air. Every parent knows when his child is in love, however forbidden the alliance. Every spouse whose husband or wife has a lover, real or longed for, sees that lover's form, soon or eventually, at the table at breakfast, in the car as they drive to market, between them in their bed. Love manifests itself in dailiness. Estrangement seeks shadow, flees the mirror, pretends to muteness and does not answer its name when called. It has taken a lifetime, for example, to be able to say of Justin and myself, "We simply do not get along," but of course that does not capture the magnitude of our rupture.

Since Father's funeral, my brother and I have not spoken. But that silence is merely the confirmation of our breach. I was five years old when Mother got pregnant. She would have me sit beside her and place my hand on her belly.

"Now, Karl," she would say, "this is your new brother or sister, we don't know which, but we'll love either one just the same, won't we?"

Beneath my palm, the sexless stranger moved. I pulled my hand away as if a shark had stirred in those waters beneath my mother's skirt. What would be expected of me? Already I had distanced from my brother, and he was not yet born. I remember the day of his birth. We had finished our dinner. Father was in his overstuffed chair in the parlor, reading the *Saturday*

Evening Post. My mother saved the Norman Rockwell covers in a cardboard chest she kept under her bed.

"When I have a sewing room," she'd say, "I'll frame the best ones and hang them on the walls. When we have our house."

Now she was in the kitchen, washing the dishes, her great mound of a stomach making it difficult for her to reach the spigot. I sat at the table, coloring, when suddenly the pot she was struggling to rinse flew from her hands and bounced off the stove, clattering finally to the floor like a great clanging bell announcing some royal event.

"Wendell!" she screamed. "Get ready to go!"

Somewhere in the rush of leaving, my father carried me—carried me!—because my five-year-old gait was not efficient enough now in this emergency, or festival, I was not sure which, to the Beckers' apartment two floors down. A friendly couple who spent most of each day and evening playing alternating games of backgammon and checkers—"One for challenge," Mr. Becker had explained, "one for relaxation"—I felt comfortable enough in their rooms. Indeed, I was there a week later again, when Father brought Mother and Justin home. Through the latticework of a weeping cherry, I watched the Nash we had then pull up to the building. It did not look to me like our car any longer. With Mother away, and the baby's arrival imminent and pervasive, objects I had lived with all the five years of my rather solemn life grew strange to me, changed hues, altered shape and size.

Everything I knew moved imperceptibly away from me. I veered toward isolation now, as a car whose steering demands an extra tug on the wheel to keep its vehicle in its designated lane. I was separate now, separate from my parents and this baby I was taught to call "brother," whose name was Justin, whose cry was tyrannical, whose eyes gazed upon me as a hunter observes his prey—the impassive gaze through the gunsight, that stillness before vengeance. As if in the intelligence of his infancy, he knew I begrudged his presence, retaliation became the preoccupation of his childhood, the drama of his manhood.

I did not truly perceive the depth of our mutual antagonism until I was fifteen and Justin was ten. Although we shared a bedroom, although the sound of my brother's breathing still infiltrates my dreams, although much of my boyhood involved keeping clear of Justin's mischief, still I did not understand its range until that Saturday afternoon when we went together to the zoo. It was balmy after days of rain, the kind of weather that summons boys into the sun-christened air.

Father had gone to the Bureau. At breakfast, he'd said, "I am working on a big case, a major case in American crime."

Mother set the platter of pancakes on the table. "In American crime prevention, Wendell. You'll have the boys thinking you're in the rackets just because you're careless with your grammar."

"Wish he was," Justin said.

"Was what?" said Mother.

"In the rackets. A hood. I saw a show about Al Capone, he—"

We all stared at Justin. He grinned. Mother said,

"Your father is in law enforcement and we are all very proud of his work. Apologize."

Justin made a noise like a machine gun.

Mother set her hands on her hips, her face reddened, her cheeks puffed out—she looked as if she were inflating, adding size, readying for battle with her disobedient boy. But Father directed his criminologist's gaze on Justin, took him in as one might take in Exhibit A in court.

"Karl, your brother doesn't seem to be able to handle himself today, so I'd like you to take care of him. Find some project that will engage his mind as well as his body."

Justin quieted down, appeared almost docile. He had not yet reached the point in his boyhood when he would argue directly with Father. And yet they were always adversaries. At Father's funeral, Justin's anger would vie with death itself for attention.

"We could go to the zoo," I said that earlier morning. I looked at my brother. "I could take you to see the snakes."

"Don't put it like he has a choice," Mother said. "This is the punishment, remember."

In the snake house, I knocked on the door marked AUTHORIZED PERSONNEL ONLY, and Mr. Peabody, the herpetologist whose friendship I had cultivated, opened the door to Justin and me.

"I'd like you to meet my brother," I said to the tall, spectacled man, his sandy hair cut close to his scalp in the manner of a Marine. He had been a Marine in World War II.

"After what I saw," he'd told me once, "I knew I didn't want to spend much time with people anymore.

"I wouldn't know about that," I had said. But I did.

Now he said, "Well, well, another Fry. I didn't know you had a brother, Karl."

I realized I had never talked about my family to Mr. Peabody at all, and he had never asked, or mentioned his to me. We came singly to each other, without attachments. Years later, Charlotte would say, "You recognized each other's loneliness," and I imagine she was correct. Behind the cages that housed the snakes the public came to see, Mr. Peabody had his laboratory where he treated sick reptiles and studied healthy ones.

"Well, he does have a brother," Justin said.

You would not have known it. We don't resemble each other at all.

I am fair, thick-waisted, my shoulders so sloped one might think weights had been attached to them in infancy. In shape and pallor, I resemble a yellow squash. This dumpiness—for that is the social judgment on my natural state—always struck me less as a handicap than a statement: *Karl Fry will not engage in games of sport or seduction.*

That was the message my body conveyed to me. Whereas Justin did push-ups in his crib before infants are even expected to raise their heads; his bones and muscles are assembled with a sculptor's sense of proportion. People always remarked on the striking contrast of his dark hair and skin to his glacier-blue eyes. Yet he has been less happy in his handsomeness than I in my unremarkable, even laughable, looks.

I saw a picture once of Charlotte's former husband. He was lean and suave; he radiated fitness. He reminded me of the men who model for *Esquire* magazine, wearing their clothes and success and women with equal flair.

"What do you see in me?" I asked her, shaken by Raymond's polished image.

"I see you," she said. "I don't see a mask or a costume. In my Chicago life—it seems like another life to me, now—what passed for beauty was disguise. All the money we spent on it. All the hours. I had a friend who would sneak out of bed in the morning before the alarm went off so she could put on her makeup before her husband woke up. He had never even seen her without her makeup, Karl. Raymond never thought I did enough with myself. I realized after a few years that I would never be sufficiently illusory for him. I was still too real. A broken nail, a run in my hose, a stain on my blouse: How he would chafe at these reminders that I was imperfect. Human. Don't you think there's a kind of hysteria in all this 'youth and beauty' business? It makes me sad. When I was married to Raymond, it just made me anxious—how could I master it all?—but now it makes me sad. I think you are very beautiful, Karl Fry, now that I can see again."

About Justin and me, Charlotte had said, "I don't think you two have ever really seen each other. You've always looked at one another through anger, and anger distorts everything."

Certainly that day in the snake house, the anger was there as surely as if a wall of rippled glass were suspended between us. When Justin looked at me, what

[189]

monster appeared to him in my clothes? What enemy who called himself "brother"?

In the white-tile-walled laboratory, Mr. Peabody led us from cage to cage, describing the snakes housed in the mesh-doored wooden boxes. Through the fine screening, we could see each serpent coiled in its nest, seemingly oblivious to its confinement. The poisonous snakes did not look different from the benign ones. Nothing in their gaze or the twist of their bodies, nothing evident in their markings, indicated which were venomous, which friendly. I had had this tour before, but Justin had never been here. He paid close attention to Mr. Peabody's information. He looked each snake in the eye, as if he were having a silent conversation with each. I had never seen him so focused before, so interested in one thing for so long a time. Justin had always been restless, even in babyhood. Give him a rattle, he'd turn it over in his hand and throw it on the floor. In the midst of building a tower of blocks, he'd abandon that project, scribble a few lines on a piece of paper, rip it up in displeasure, open up the Tinker Toys and spill the pieces across the rug. This jumpiness carried over into his school work. Teachers were always writing on his report cards: "Concentration problems." But he did not have such a problem in the snake house.

"Now here," said Mr. Peabody and reached into one of the cages, "here is a California king snake. Non-poisonous." He held up the black-and-white reptile. "They make good pets."

I was examining the California king, when Justin said, "How about this one? Does this one make a good pet, too?"

We turned to face him; he was on haunches on the table on the other side of the room. He had opened the door to the cage beside him, and the snake it housed was slithering across the room.

"Now don't anybody move," Mr. Peabody said, and he reached behind him for a long-handled net that hung on the wall. If the snake had not been poisonous, he would have reached for it with his hands. I opened my mouth to cry out, but the year-old timbre in my voice was gone; my words sounded like chirps, like a sparrow's thin cries for help. My hands were white flags raised in surrender.

"This," said Mr. Peabody, "is a copperhead."

He said it as if he were continuing our tour, as if this were one more exhibit whose features he would describe for us. He lowered the net with such control, it seemed to be slow motion. Perhaps the air had so thickened with my fear that the net could not have moved through it any faster than it did. I was afraid of the snake and I was afraid of my brother, and I am not sure which one frightened me more.

And Justin? Was he simply a child who had opened the wrong cage? A curious boy pulling back after he realizes he has overstepped his bounds, ventured too far? Could error or mischief-gone-awry have produced the smile I saw on my brother's face as Mr. Peabody brought down the net on the snake that had already traveled half the space from prison to prey? Wasn't that the same smile I would see on his face years later as he addressed crowds of anti-war protestors from podiums all over the country?

"You don't believe in this war any more than I

do," he would tell me. "Why aren't you out on the streets with me?"

I would say, "There are many ways to protest," but what I truly meant was: *I will no longer be controlled by the smile of power.*

And when he called me from his hiding place, breaking months of silence, a warrant out for his arrest on perjury charges, our parents drained, should I have then capitulated to his proscription: "Remember, I called you, not them. Not a word to them. They'll have to wait it out." I could not allow them to continue to suffer. That Father chose to act on the knowledge I provided— that I did not foresee. You will not believe me, Justin, but I did not foresee it. I did not foresee it.

As soon as the copperhead was netted, Justin leapt from his perch and bounded out the door.

"He probably scared himself half to death," Mr. Peabody said, putting the snake back in its cage. He was not even ruffled. He seemed to have even enjoyed showing off his skills in the face of danger. Still a Marine, my gentle friend, even though he had removed himself as far as he could from battles, military and otherwise. He looked at me.

"Why, you've lost your color," he said, and I felt like a turtle marooned on its own back, my mouth flapping in mute distress. "There wasn't a thing to fear, Karl. I'm prepared for all eventualities in here. Why, even if one of us had been bitten—"

What if he did it on purpose?

The unspoken words were cinders in my eyes. I lurched from the laboratory before the tears betrayed me.

Years later, at my brother's trial, his arrest arranged by our father as another man might engineer a son's admission to a prestigious graduate school, Justin looked at me with the same question lodged in his gaze: *What if you did it on purpose, Karl? What if you did it on purpose?*

If I had put that question to him in the snake house, would he have answered as I answered him, as I answer him still in dreams, in imagined conversations?

I did not foresee it. I did not foresee it. I did not foresee it.

I hear the two of us, in chorus, chanting expiation.

In the bright noise of the crowded zoo, Justin was waiting for me out front. He had climbed atop a trash can formed like a hippopotamus, his spindly child-legs wrapped around the hippo's giant neck.

"Come down," I said.

My voice seemed to disappear down the hippo's cavernous mouth. I raised my eyes to Justin, and he was armored in sunlight.

"Justin, I said—"

"I heard you," he said, finally sliding down the beast's back to the ground, where I stood trembling in the afternoon heat.

We did not speak on the walk home, or during the rest of the afternoon. I lay on my bed for several hours in a trance of diminishing terror. By dinner, the quaking had ceased and my color had returned.

Father said, "And what did you boys do with yourselves today?"

I wanted to tell him the truth. But what was the truth? That Justin had accidentally released the copperhead? That my brother's resentment of me had culminated in a murderous act on his part? Justin eyed me. What good would it do me if I told? Father would punish Justin, either for carelessness or malevolence, whichever he chose to believe. But that would not alter the fact that what had occurred in the snake house was an event in the lives of my brother and me; it belonged only to the two of us. No one could guarantee peace between us, as no one could engender love.

"We went to the zoo," I said.

Justin served himself another helping of mashed potatoes.

Mother said, "You see what a good dose of healthy activity will do for a boy's appetite."

"Amen," said Father. "Amen to that."

I have come a far way, Mother, from that dinner table. In that household I always felt we acted out one life while another one went on in the air, above our heads. There, our real natures whispered like ghosts the true stories of apartment 106.

Karl: "I think Justin might have tried to kill me once."

Justin: "Karl never wanted a brother at all and I'll punish him for that."

Wendell: "Rose, you are a disappointing wife to me."

Rose: "Wendell, my dreams are all cramped up in this place; they can't breathe anymore."

When we arrived at the Lodge from the airport, I wanted to tell you: *Breathe here, Mother. Here no ghosts are swallowing up the air. In this house, we live in our flesh. Every word is whole, not crumb or sliver of what we mean. The garden you dreamed of grows in the soil on which this house rests. I plant the seedlings for you, as well as for myself.*

Traveling down for the wedding was too much for Mother. She went to bed before dinner. After we did the dishes, Mary took her bath and I settled in the living room to work on the toast I'd deliver that very hour at the reception. When she brought me a glass of iced tea, I said to Charlotte, "We haven't been close for so long, my daughter and me." Pain swelled in my chest, my throat.

Charlotte said, "I think you'll be able to get to know her all over again, now that she's getting married."

Charlotte's daughter will never get married.

Charlotte has known this since Mary was two years old and the doctor confirmed what her parents already suspected: that Mary was "slow." Charlotte told me he said it the way one might refer to a clock that didn't keep time properly. He suggested they put her away and get themselves a new child, much in the manner one trades in faulty cars. Although he talked of "alternative residential modes" and "extended-care facilities," Charlotte heard warehouse, junk heap, dump.

The doctor said, "If you keep her with you, you will come to resent the burden and it will poison all the other parts of your life." The faces of his healthy children smiled at Charlotte and Raymond from photographs on the console behind the doctor's desk. "Don't you agree?" he said.

When I rode to this hospital in the ambulance, Diana's blood bright on my own hand, her name a word she did not understand, or hear, I knew finally how Charlotte had suffered. Her memories churned in me as if they were my own, part of the white-water river I ride even as I stand here on the solid tile floor, even as the clock beneath which the nurse sits claims that only the present exists.

"You're already exhausted," Raymond had said to her. "I come home every day and you're ready to drop, Charlotte." He fingered his silk tie, sharpened the crease on his Brooks Brothers suit pants. He tried to sound sympathetic, as if his concern were for her, for her fatigue. But she saw the anger contained in the set of his mouth, in the nerve that twitched in his cheek. It was true: She was exhausted. She struggled through dinner, fell asleep as soon as Mary finished her nine o'clock bottle, and if Raymond reached for her in bed, later, she lay numb and stiff beneath him, her real self hiding in the dreams she had not yet finished and would return to "when Raymond finished with my body."

One night she could not sleep. Shadows thickened and moved toward her from the walls. The air-conditioning hissed through the floorboard vents. Moonlight bled through the curtains. She put her palm on

Raymond's back: It rose and fell indifferently. She swung her legs to the floor, picked her way over the ghostly terrain down the thickly-carpeted hallway to the bathroom. She swallowed two sleeping pills. Perched on the edge of the tub, she waited for the panic to pale. In the mirror, finally, her face came back to her like a friend she hadn't seen in years.

In this drugged daze of well-being, she floated into Mary's room. There in her crib, her daughter lay peacefully in her slow sleep—Charlotte said she imagined Mary's blood barely stirring through her veins, her heart stilled to the slightest quiver. Above her bed, paper birds hovered, stopped in flight, treading air. Even the clock seemed to tick less insistently there, keeping its own time, refusing to rush from one hour to the next. Charlotte settled herself on the floor of her slow child's room, and when Raymond found his wife there in the morning, he said, as if she were being arrested for vagrancy: "Charlotte, you are falling apart. I think you need a complete rest."

It was how he said "complete" that informed her of his true intentions.

"You aren't speaking of Bermuda," she said. "Are you?"

As if she were one of his clients at the brokerage firm in which he was already a partner, as if he were advising her on a complex stock transaction, her first husband said, "Charlotte, in this situation, a more controlled environment is required. You'll understand that once you begin to feel better."

"That was the moment my marriage ended," she

told me. She said she heard it break in two as surely as she heard the front door close behind Raymond once he left for work. Then she packed all their clothes, Mary's and hers, stuffed the diaper bag with Pampers, bottles, rubber toys and rattles. She folded up the canvas stroller, took a taxi to O'Hare Airport, and not until they were in the terminal did she realize she had no idea where they were going.

Mounted in midair, screens announced arrivals and departures. It seemed to Charlotte that everyone in the world was leaving one place for another, that all other human activity was peripheral to this one: escape. In her stroller, Mary gazed at the names as if they were star constellations: San Francisco, Houston, Montreal. They might as well have been planning to travel into space, for all the comfort those names held for Charlotte that day. She tried to imagine herself in one city, then another, but each fantasy began with a plummet, she and Mary free-falling through the colorless air. Then Miami: Charlotte had visited there as a child. She remembered smells, she summoned up from those days the feel of a palm tree's trunk, the texture of the fronds she'd hidden in when she'd been small. Little else returned, but it was enough to seem like the promise of solid ground beneath them.

An hour later they were boarding the plane, and soon Chicago disappeared as if it had slipped off the earth, as if it had never existed at all.

They had lived in Miami for thirteen years when Charlotte and I found each other. When we met, it was as if

we had lost each other once and had now retrieved what
had been important to us. How else to explain our immediate relief at one another's presence? I was nothing
like the boys at Evanston High that Charlotte had dated
as a girl, or the Northwestern fraternity men with whom
she'd danced, gotten drunk, driven with to coves along
Lake Michigan's northern shore, the windows of the car
steaming over as they necked so that when they rose,
panting and sweaty, it was as if they had wound up
underwater, drowned without knowing it, slid silently
into the lake in the midst of their frenzied couplings. Of
course, they hadn't drowned at all. In ten minutes, they
were tidy and combed again, his shirt tucked in, her
blouse buttoned.

I was nothing like Raymond, either, whose grad-
uate-school finesse convinced Charlotte on their fourth
date to forsake the cramped Ford sedan for a motel room
and with each garment of hers he removed, she imagined a promise being offered: "I'll get a job with a class-
A firm" (blouse); "we'll have an apartment on the Gold
Coast" (skirt); "a Bermuda honeymoon" (bra); and
"beautiful, beautiful children" (panties, garter belt, hose).
They made love to the future more than to each other.
They were in love with luck, with entitlement. Later
Raymond took her to a Chinese restaurant, and after
their meal, he ordered two dozen fortune cookies. They
cracked them all open, she said, saving those messages
that verified their plans. On that foundation—sturdy as
air, solid as words, deep as Raymond's ready Colgate
smile and impervious slate-gray eyes—they married.

So who was this other man, years later, in an

out-of-shape Banlon jersey and baggy trousers he kept hitching up at the waist as if he feared they'd fall to his ankles and leave him exposed in his boxer shorts? Charlotte was sure I'd wear boxer shorts, and I did. I was overweight, my hair unruly, my complexion pale, yet I was the first man since she'd left Raymond towards whom Charlotte felt that release of affection and need which she so feared and desired.

As for me: I believe I lived in some sort of sleep state from which Charlotte woke me. She revived me. She did not save my life as much as lead me to it.

"May I help you?" she said, because I had come into Gordon's Pharmacy where she worked the front register: discount on medicines, no night hours and half her health insurance paid.

"Pictures for Fry," I said.

"Pictures."

"Photographs," I said, as if she hadn't understood. "I brought them in last week."

She flipped through the envelopes in the wooden box beside the register.

"Here you are," she said. "I advise you to look through them, to make sure you haven't been charged for more than turned out." She said this in a conspiratorial whisper. She flashed me a political smile.

"Good idea," I said, and removed the photographs from their container.

She rested her elbows on the counter and leaned forward. She smelled clean. Her eyes said, "I know sorrow." Her mouth said, "But I am not bitter."

"May I see your pictures, Mr. Fry?" she said.

I flushed. "Well, I—certainly, if you're interested."

I spread them out before us.

"Most of these are of my daughter, Diana," I said. "She's fifteen."

Charlotte looked at the beautiful girl in the white eyelet dress, an orchid pinned on her shoulder, her golden hair heavy on her bare shoulders.

"That was the prom," I said. "She's very—popular. Too much so, I fear."

I smoothed out my forehead with my hand, as if to erase the distress I knew Charlotte had observed, as if I had committed a betrayal of some sort.

"I have a daughter the same age," she said. "She's retarded. She's not like your girl at all."

Who was I, a stranger, that she should lay her daughter's condition before me as if it were a calling card, a glove dropped discreetly at my toe? But I saw embarrassment unsteady her, and my mistrust yielded.

"In the ways that count, we are all alike," I said, holding her in my gaze because I knew she was dizzy and could fall down on the floor without my support.

Sometimes, Charlotte says, she fears my nature will carry me away from this world, to a monastery perhaps, an island of my own, a retreat from this sullied place. She will have to remain here.

"I'm not as pure as you," she says. "I cut deals when I have to. Raymond taught me how to drive a hard bargain."

About Fry's Lodge, I always say, "My wife is the businesswoman. I attend to the grounds and cabins, but Charlotte advertises, talks to the bank, orders supplies, decides when we have to raise the rates."

Did Diana turn into such a wild girl to shock me out of my solitude, to make me say things I'd regret, go on a drinking spree, smash plates to the floor?

Through everything, I have stayed calm. Have I been wise? In the face of Florence's tirades, in response to Charlotte's urgings that I get my daughter professional help, I have insisted, "Be patient." Even now, hours after the shooting, I can still see the spot in the distance towards which Diana has been traveling to a new life. I do see it. As if there were truly a map of the earth on which people's lives were plotted like rivers and roads, cities through which to pass, countries whose languages must be mastered, strange and twisted routes towards far-off destinations.

Think of me as a traveler.

Even though I have never visited the places in the world where tourists go; even though I walk the grounds each morning as if it will take me the rest of my life to know this limited terrain; even though I am happiest working in the garden I have planted out back of my own house, making each square inch of soil my own; still I journey as far as men who hop on jets to foreign lands, who use passports the way I use my Dade County library card, whose all-leather American Touristers are always packed for last-minute flights while my plaid canvas Samsonite gathers dust in the back of our closet.

Two long days ago, Charlotte was hanging clothes in the yard. I walked back from the morning round of cabins. I heard Diana's voice, and Mother's. Though I could not distinguish words, the cadences were so similar, it was as if I were hearing one woman with fluctuating pitch. As I walked up the slope to the driveway I saw how their bodies, too, resembled each other, a certain forward tilt in each woman's bearing, a readiness that suggested movement even as they both stood still. Charlotte says she used to be like that herself: set to bound at the slightest provocation. Raymond called it "vitality," but Charlotte recognized it for the skittishness it was: some discomfort always at her back, prodding her when she slagged, rewarding her sprints in a race she took to be her obligation. She came to learn otherwise. In place, we are explorers; at rest, we journey far.

"Look who's here!" Mother called.

She hugged Diana. I had tried to hug my daughter for a year or more after the divorce, but each time I touched her, she flinched away. Finally she acquiesced, but there was such defeat in her body, I stopped pursuing her. When I married Charlotte and we moved here, I hoped Diana would feel at home with me again—I prayed she would—but she withdrew even further. When I saw her yield to Mother, return love with love, I had to hold on to a tree to keep myself from running to them, pulling my child—how I miss my child!—into my own embrace.

Just then, Mary appeared on the porch. She was waving both arms like a person stranded on an island who's flagging down a rescuing boat.

"Di!" she yelled. "Di! Di!"

As if she were oblivious to Mary's greeting, Diana opened the driver's door of her red Chevette and burrowed into her seat. Mary kept calling her, but Diana had already started the engine. Like a woman caught in cross fire, Mother ducked, held her hat to her head, veered towards the car, then abruptly shifted directions and strode to the porch. I watched her give Mary a hug and a kiss. This quieted the girl, though she looked confused as anyone would whose affection for one person is responded to by another.

Yet hasn't my mother been doing that all her life? Giving Justin and me the attention we craved from Father. Speaking to one son on behalf of another, standing in for the absent one. Creating a kind of family-by-proxy, as if that were ever possible.

Love requires encounter.

When we married, I gave Charlotte as a wedding gift a leather-bound copy of Martin Buber's *I And Thou*, and we read it aloud to each other for several nights. Over our beds hangs a line she embroidered with gold thread on a piece of white silk: "All real living is meeting."

Mother returned to the car; she and Diana drove off.

I walked from the place where I had been witness to the porch on which Mary wept.

Thursday afternoon. The heat pressed like a great sweaty
palm on the house. In the parlor, I sat at Charlotte's
desk and the polished wood carried its own coolness, as
if Charlotte's presence were alive in the wood she had
refinished herself.

"Dear Diana—"

I began again the letter I had started many times
over the years, but had never finished. I could hear the
words imploring, "Forgive me, forgive me," and I cringed
at that plea. I discussed this once with Charlotte. "Why
shouldn't I ask her to forgive me? Why am I being so
prideful? What keeps me—"

"First you must forgive yourself," she said. "You
can't ask Diana to do that for both of you."

Now the phone rang. I set down the pen. A silent caller, although the sounds of an airport were au-
dible. Perhaps I was meant to listen to that jet whine;
perhaps the flight calls held a message for me. Last week
we had eaten Chinese food at the Golden Palace and my
fortune read, "You will take a long journey." We had
laughed. It has always been enough for me to know the
earth is spinning through space. Given that, staying put
may be the one true adventure.

"Is anybody there?" I said.

Nothing but noise. Cacophony. My caller hung
up.

Again, I returned to my letter. Over the years,

I had probably discarded a ream of paper, each page the first sentences of the message to my daughter I could not compose.

How long had Mother tried to tell me about her father's suicide? How many times had she rehearsed the speech she failed to deliver, or dreamed the talk we never had, until this week? Her accomplishment inspired me. At first I did not see how her confiding in me resembled my need to communicate with Diana. Mother spoke of her girlhood, of tragic events that occurred before I even existed. My need has been to explain to Diana the circumstances of her parents' divorce, the sundering of her family. To share with her the reasons I could not remain with Florence even though leaving would throw my child's life into upheaval. But as I did my chores this morning—changing the guests' bed linens, restocking tissue and soap, fixing the window in number 4, spraying the weeds that sprout like whiskers from the sandy ground behind the cabins—I saw how Mother was speaking to me of my childhood as much as her own, how she was lifting from my shoulders a burden I had borne without knowing it, as Diana bears my guilt without knowing it.

"Dear Diana," I wrote. "This morning as I gardened, Grandmother Rose confided in me, and I saw what a gift it is for a parent to entrust a grown child with such secrets, however sorrowful their nature."

Sorrow. Now I understood those times when Mother's eyes would shimmer suddenly, as if a smoke bomb had been let loose in the room. I saw her tears and pretended I did not. I invented my own responsibility for them. Wasn't I more important to her than Father or Justin? Wasn't it obvious that I was the source of her pain? As for the events in her past which might have caused her present distress—well, I could barely conceive of my mother existing in the world before me. In bed, I would think, "I'll be a better son," and vow to overcome my shyness, my sickliness, my inability to carry a tune—whatever it was about my young character that burdened her so. In time, I ceased hunting for the precise weakness in myself that had injured her. I came to accept, even ignore, the suffering that flashed like a tic across her face.

But when she told me about John Temple's suicide, I felt the relief of one who has puzzled over the riddle of the Sphinx all his life and has finally been given the answer. My brain chanted to me: "If only I had known, if only I had known." Known what? Known the truth about the grandfather whose picture still sits on Mother's dresser, between her hand-painted lamp and her bronze music box, inside of which a porcelain ballerina pirouettes twenty-seven times to Brahm's "Lullaby"? His face gazes out of an oval frame of ornate filigree Mother bought many years ago for two dollars at a church bazaar.

"This is perfect for my father," she had said, bringing out a box of faded sepia prints from her bottom dresser drawer.

I was eight years old. It was then I realized that Mother had never talked about her father before. Her mother had died when I was two; relatives from West Virginia sent Christmas cards and once a year a contingent trekked to Washington, as if to check out yet again the odd girl cousin who had left Berkeley Springs and ensconced herself in the middle of traffic and crime. But a father?

"What was he like?"

She trimmed the photograph to fit the frame. Scraps of John Temple's jacket littered our kitchen table. "He was—lively," she said. "He liked jokes."

He was smiling at me from behind the glass, as if he had made his way to our apartment and was peering in on us through a window. I smiled back. It seemed nicer to have a grandfather than not. But all the years that followed that day, I never thought that this grinning man had anything important to do with me.

If only I had known. That Mother mourned John Temple, and not my failings. That loneliness ran in the family, and I was not an aberration in the Fry/Temple clan, but my grandfather's direct descendent: solitary, unmoored, given to dreams of transforming death, my soul ascending like a feather or a leaf borne upwards on currents of golden air. How I struggled to be Wendell Fry's child or Rose Fry's child, when all along—with no struggle required—I was John Temple's boy, a generation removed. Hadn't I come close to taking his very route?

I had just driven home from the Safeway where I had gone for a loaf of pumpernickel bread. I do not like white bread at all, yet Florence insisted on buying it exclusively, as if her childhood customs took precedence over mine, her tastes the result of a superior upbringing resulting in superior habits. At a red light, I had opened the cellophane and the bread's aroma—something like clay, or earth after a rain—made me cry. Even after the light turned green and the car behind me bleated its horn at me, I'd remained in place, weeping, a piece of pumpernickel bread crumbling in the grip of my hand. The car I was blocking whipped around me, the driver hurling me a look somewhere between disgust and stupefaction. It was enough to return me to the flow of traffic, but I had driven through the glare of my own tears, as if I were driving through a blinding rain; and the bread's smell grew so potent, I thought I might suffocate from its pungent odor. I saw my hand on the steering wheel. But I could not feel its familiar form against my palm. My foot, too, was numb, and I lost any sense of how much pressure I was exerting on the gas pedal. Where was my body? I hardly realized I had drifted across the center line, even as the headlights of the oncoming car bore down on me like two suns. We did not crash. The other driver whipped into the curb lane in which, blessedly, no other car traveled.

"You could have killed us both!" he screamed at me through his window as I returned to the proper side of the road. I thought, *Of course, that was my intention*, recognizing it for the first time.

His indictment and my unspoken reply repeated themselves like jingles on the radio for the rest of my drive home. By the time the car was safely garaged, I was nothing but that couplet: "You could have killed us both."/"Of course, that was my intention." I bore it into the house with me.

"I think I tried to kill myself, Florence."

She was in the kitchen, laying a floor of Sears stick-on white bricklike tile on top of the faded linoleum that she had hated from the day we'd moved into the house nine years before. Diana was already asleep; it was nearly ten o'clock.

"Florence," I repeated, "I think I tried to kill myself."

She did not look up from the tile she had softened in the oven and was now trimming with her sewing shears.

She said, "Cuts like butter," ripped off the backing from the piece and placed it adhesive-side down in the corner for which it had been cut.

I said, "I drove over the center line, Florence."

She was on her knees, pressing on the tile with the tips of her fingers. She looked as if she might be preparing for a handstand.

She said, "I wonder if brick-red would have been a better choice."

In my letter to Diana, I wrote, "Your mother and I were never suited to each other. We did not know each other. We did not know ourselves. I took my idea of 'Wife' and placed it like a cloak over the real person your mother was. She had her notion of 'Husband' and wrapped me in it. This is not uncommon, but always tragic. As for me, at the time, I was glad to be in disguise. I did not think much of myself then, though I believe I hid that very well from people, myself included."

Outside, the jeep rattled over the stones. Charlotte signaled to me with the horn. I left my letter, still unfinished, to help her bring in the groceries. But I was writing the final version at last. I had found the words to speak to my daughter at last. I had given them to Mother a day before—"It was brave of you to remember this"—and now I offered myself the same charge, the same salute.

Thursday night. Everyone else in the house was asleep. Charlotte, Mary, my mother. The house rode through the night on currents of their breath. I walked from room to room like a sailor on watch duty. "Keep us safe, protect us from surprise attack." My daughter slept eight miles away, but she could have been on the other side of the earth.

It was not until I met Charlotte, not until love guided me to myself, that I understood I should have been the one to raise Diana. I had relinquished her to her mother as one bypasses the last serving of potatoes, or a single item reduced for quick sale. I was raised to be a gentleman.

My mother used to say, "Good deportment is your ticket to the top."

My father: "Breeding opens doors." I took their advice further than they had meant. I gave up my place in line. I held the door open for others, and Florence took Diana out one such door. I have been two steps behind my child ever since. On the screened porch overlooking my backyard garden, I brought my unfinished letter and my pen to the oilcloth-covered table where we like to eat our breakfasts, when the air is not heavy yet with heat.

I turned on the light and mosquitoes flung themselves against the screening. What was out there in the darkness that in order to escape it they would impale themselves on the mesh?

I could not make out the crickets' garble.

I did not understand the mutterings of the ocean.

At 2:00 A.M., Mary woke up screaming "Di! Di!" and then some private language I could not make out. We shook her awake, but the terror woke with her, turned her hands to clamps locked around Charlotte's wrists.

"You've had a bad dream, sweetheart," Charlotte said. "You've had a nightmare. Mother's with you now. Mother's here."

But Mary was not soothed. She called out Diana's name again and again in her sirenlike wail.

Was she remembering her stepsister's visit yesterday morning, how Diana refused to get out of the car and offer Mary the simplest exchange? Mary has suffered so many affronts in her life. Sometimes I fear that all these hurts have gathered inside her like lobbed grenades that failed to detonate, and one day this stockpile will explode in a burst of rage and grief we will be helpless to control. In the predawn dark, I shuddered that I might be witnessing the first tremors of that blast.

As if she knew I was misconstruing her fright, she struggled to speak clearly. "Di hurt," she said.

Charlotte said, "Oh, Mary! You've had one of your—experiences!"

My wife looked at me in alarm. Mary released Charlotte's wrists. She leaned against her mother as if a weight had been lifted. Mary is like a blind person whose other senses grow more acute to compensate for the lack of vision; Mary's empathy travels where her limited intelligence cannot go. In her sleep, she flew to Diana's cry before Charlotte or I had any knowledge of my daughter's plight. In her dream, Mary entered her stepsister's pain and breathed it in and made it her own.

This had happened before, Mary sensing a family member's distress before any conventional signal—phone call, pounding on the door, distraught letter—had been sounded. Once we found her weeping over Raymond's picture, the father she had not seen in years. But his support payments had continued, always on time, except for this month, his check to Charlotte weeks late. Nothing would solace Mary until Charlotte picked up the phone.

"This is a personal matter," Charlotte told his secretary. "About his daughter."

Put on "hold," Charlotte was talking suddenly to one of Raymond's partners. "Ray's got a bad drinking problem, Charlotte," he told her. "He's drying out in Boston. I can give you the number there. It's a decent place, discreet."

Mary had known before Charlotte. The child had journeyed to the father's side in that substratum beneath the surface of conscious knowledge, traveled through that underground maze of psychic tunnels only the bravest hearts can navigate.

Several years ago Mary had "found" Charlotte in

that way. Her mother had gone downtown for a day of errands. In the midst of lunch at home, Mary began screaming Charlotte's name, a litany of panic I could not quell. Only hours later would I discover that my wife had been stung by a wasp and suffered an allergic reaction. She had not been able to breathe; her throat had swollen shut. At the time of Mary's outburst Charlotte was being rushed to Mt. Sinai Hospital in the back of an ambulance.

And now Diana. Suddenly the room was spinning with lights. At the front door, two policemen, behind whom an armada of parked patrol cars flashed "emergency" over and over in the bug-ridden darkness, pounded for entry.

"What is it?" I said. My hands were cold.

One of the officers pointed towards the cabins. Their roofs glowed, as if a white fire burned in each small house. "Cabin three," he said. "A Cutler boy is holding your daughter at gunpoint, sir."

He spoke without emotion. He looked like a young Raymond, a forbidding symmetry to his features, a waxy manufactured quality from which I wanted to flee. But I stepped forward, into the doorway, as if to challenge his cool recital of those awful facts. His arm rose to bar me.

"We can't let you leave this house," he said. "We're asking you all to stay put for your own safety."

I kept my arm around Charlotte's shoulder. I felt her trembling against me.

Raymond's double looked past us into the living room. "If we could get some information—"

As if even our furniture held clues to the violence by which we were suddenly defined. What could he know of this family, of all we had suffered, of how each of us struggled to make our way in the world? Would he slash open the sofa and the antique chairs whose new covers Charlotte had needlepointed herself? Would he pry up floorboards, overturn drawers, drill holes in the walls, looking for his precious information?

I wanted to yell, "Get out of my house! We don't need you here!" as if it were the police who had brought danger to our lives; my daughter's life in jeopardy because this man, and not the one who held the gun, was here.

"She's a hostage," I heard myself say, some small part of my brain dictating the truth the larger part resisted. "Diana's—oh! My God! My dear God!"

In the hospital lobby now, my mother still with Diana, I see myself as if in a three-way mirror.

In the left panel, my father curls in a crib on the day before his death, and I maintain my vigil of a decade ago, duty stronger than disappointment, but in my face a vacancy I recognize now as loss already sustained.

Who does not grieve for the parent in one's midst, the mate in one's bed, the child in one's arms, the sibling by one's side?

In the right panel, Justin seems dead, but I watch myself watch his rib cage rise and fall almost imperceptibly beneath his regulation hospital gown. He is twenty-eight years old again. I have come again to see him in the detoxification ward of Sibley Hospital. A court of law has sentenced him to health, though he would not agree with my interpretation of the verdict. I come prepared for pain, tremors, hallucinations, rantings that make no sense. Not for this slumber from which my voice does not rouse his. He looks like a boy, frail, no older than his own small son. My legs buckle. I sit down on the chair beside my brother's bed, and weep.

The center panel holds me where I stand right now, twenty feet from my daughter's side, the seated nurse's cap caught in the frame that captures my ashen image. I could be taken for an old man today. I look like a patient myself, someone who has wandered into the wrong wing and cannot wend his way back through the maze of corridors and stairwells to the bed on which his own chart hangs, where at night he dreams his own life over and over as Diana must be dreaming hers all these hours of her drugged sleep.

"Karl."

Am I awake? I turn from the triptych to the voice behind me. As if we were meeting for the first time, my brother offers me his hand.

"How is she?" Justin says, the pain in his face so raw, he could be the one with the gunshot wound.

I mimic the doctor. "Her vital signs are strong. We expect a complete re—"

"Karl," he said. "I'm sorry."

"Well, I—"

But I do not have the words with which to accept his compassion. Such an exchange has never been made between us. Such a bridge does not exist, spanning the rough river from whose opposite banks each of us has watched the other, the distance so great we could not even be sure whether it was enemy or friend whose form we glimpsed across that water, across that pain.

"We can talk later, Karl," Justin says.

I could not tell you if that statement suggests a future in which my brother and I will truly speak to each other. Or is he simply relieved to have me return us to the silence we chose years ago? I want to ask him how he heard about Diana and why he came here and what he hopes for now, but what would the answers tell me that I do not already know?

"I'm glad you're here," I tell him, meaning that much, knowing that much to be true. I let the weight of past and future fall. I stand in the moment, and the world is no larger than this alcove against whose bare tiled wall our shadows lean.

When Mother sees us there together, in the corridor, her sons, she reaches for the wall as if she were a pilgrim at Lourdes witnessing the miracle she has prayed for for a lifetime. On that sudden surge of faith, she lets go of all her long-borne griefs. For a moment, she is a woman living in a painless world.

"What a blessing," Mother says, reaching her sons at last. "She's opened her eyes."